CAMPAIGN 390

THE RECONQUEST OF BURMA 1944–45

From Operation *Capital* to the Sittang Bend

ROBERT LYMAN

ILLUSTRATED BY JOHNNY SHUMATE

Series editor Nikolai Bogdanovic

OSPREY PUBLISHING
Bloomsbury Publishing Plc
Kemp House, Chawley Park, Cumnor Hill, Oxford OX2 9PH, UK
29 Earlsfort Terrace, Dublin 2, Ireland
1385 Broadway, 5th Floor, New York, NY 10018, USA
E-mail: info@ospreypublishing.com
www.ospreypublishing.com

OSPREY is a trademark of Osprey Publishing Ltd

First published in Great Britain in 2023

A catalogue record for this book is available from the British Library.

ISBN: PB 9781472854063; eBook 9781472854056;
ePDF 9781472854070; XML 9781472854087

23 24 25 26 27   10 9 8 7 6 5 4 3 2 1

Maps by Bounford.com
3D BEVs by Paul Kime
Index by Alison Worthington
Typeset by PDQ Digital Media Solutions, Bungay, UK
Printed and bound in India by Replika Press Private Ltd.

MIX
Paper from
responsible sources
FSC® C016779
www.fsc.org

Readers can discover more about the work of illustrator Johnny Shumate at
the below website:

https://johnnyshumate.com

Osprey Publishing supports the Woodland Trust, the UK's leading woodland
conservation charity.

To find out more about our authors and books visit
www.ospreypublishing.com. Here you will find extracts, author
interviews, details of forthcoming events and the option to sign up for
our newsletter.

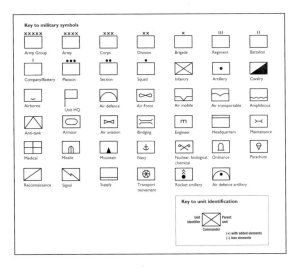

Acronyms used in this work

AFO	Anti-Fascist Organization
ALFSEA	Allied Land Forces South-East Asia
BDA	Burma Defence Army
BNA	Burma National Army
GOC	General Officer Commanding
IAF	Indian Air Force
INA	Indian National Army
NCAC	Northern Combat Area Command
RAF	Royal Air Force
SEAC	South East Asia Command
SOE	Special Operations Executive
USAAF	United States Army Air Forces

Dedication

This book is dedicated to the Kohima Educational Society (KES) in
Nagaland, India, for it was at Kohima in 1944 that the reconquest of Burma
was made possible.

When you go home
Tell them of Us
And say, for your tomorrow
We gave our today

(Epitaph on the 2nd Division Memorial, Kohima)

Front cover main illustration: Lieutenant George Knowland of
3 Commando Brigade fires at advancing Japanese troops at Hill 170,
the Arakan, 1945. (Johnny Shumate)

Title page photograph: Indian troops of 6th/7th Rajput Rifles
moving through Pyawbwe north of Rangoon, May 1945. (AFP via
Getty Images)

CONTENTS

Overall movement of Allied forces in Burma, December 1944–May 1945

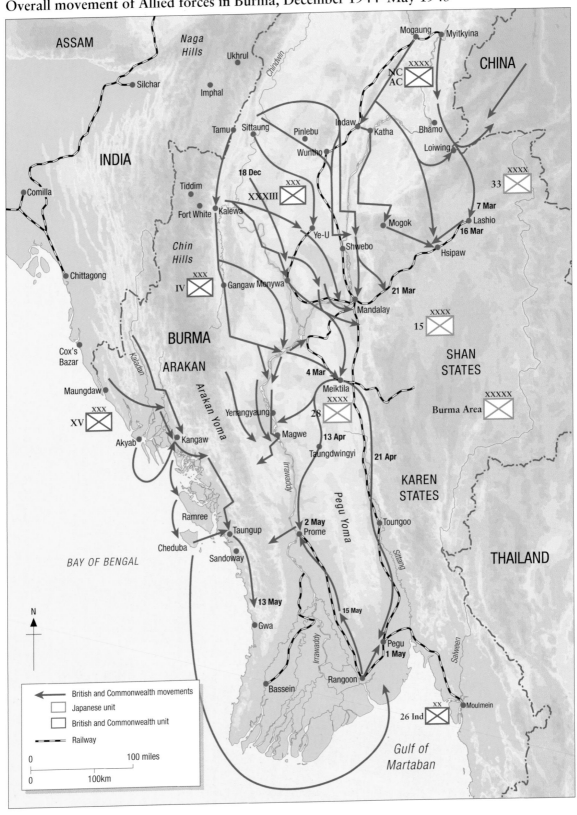

ASSAM

Naga Hills

Ukhrul

Silchar

Imphal

Chindwin

Mogaung
Myitkyina

CHINA

NC
AC

XXXX

INDIA

Tamu
Sittaung
Pinlebu
Indaw
Katha
Bhamo
Loiwing

Wuntho

Comilla

18 Dec

Tiddim

XXXIII
XXX

Fort White
Kalewa

Ye-U
Shwebo

Mogok

33
XXXX

7 Mar
Lashio
16 Mar

Chittagong

Chin Hills

IV
XXX

Gangaw
Monywa

Hsipaw

21 Mar

Mandalay

Cox's Bazar

BURMA

ARAKAN

Kaladan

Maungdaw

Arakan Yoma

XV
XXX

Yenangyaung

4 Mar

Meiktila

15
XXXX

SHAN STATES

XXXXX
Burma Area

Akyab
Kangaw

Magwe

28
XXXX

13 Apr
Taungdwingyi

21 Apr

KAREN STATES

Ramree

Taungup

2 May
Prome

Toungoo

Pegu Yoma

Sittang

THAILAND

Cheduba
Sandoway

Irrawaddy

BAY OF BENGAL

13 May

Gwa

15 May

Irrawaddy

Salween

Pegu
1 May

N

Bassein

Rangoon

26 Ind
XX
Moulmein

Gulf of Martaban

Legend:
- British and Commonwealth movements
- Japanese unit
- British and Commonwealth unit
- Railway

0 — 100 miles
0 — 100km

4

ORIGINS OF THE CAMPAIGN

The physical reconquest of Burma was not part of Allied Grand Strategy in 1944 and 1945. It happened – in 1945 – despite it. In particular, it happened because of the dramatic failure of the Japanese invasion of India – Operation *U-Go* – which ended ignominiously for the Japanese Empire in August 1944. This failure allowed Vice Admiral Louis Mountbatten, Supreme Allied Commander South-East Asia, the opportunity to follow the defeated Japanese Fifteenth Army into Burma proper. Nevertheless, even when the Chindwin River was crossed by the advancing British Fourteenth Army in December 1944, few on the Allied side gave any thought to the possibility that a successful offensive into Upper Burma could do much more than capture Mandalay. It would, it was hoped, allow the consolidation of Upper Burma, thereby to support the new Burma Road, built through the mountains by pick, shovel and American bulldozer, from Ledo. For it was China, and the Burma Road that supplied it with American war materiel, which lay at the heart of Allied strategy. The recovery of the whole of Burma was, even six months before it was achieved, considered a pipe dream.

But this didn't mean that the reconquest of Burma wasn't desired. Although never formally articulated as a British policy objective, Britain

British troops of the 36th Division, advancing south along the Railway Corridor from Mogaung in November 1944, engage a Japanese position with cup dischargers prior to an assault. This was terrain fought through by the Chinidts the previous year during Operation *Thursday*. (Victoria State Archives)

clearly wanted to recover its lost colony. The United States was never interested in Burma per se, seeing the recovery of the Burma Road – or parts of it – as concomitant to resupplying China. For Chiang Kai-shek, however, the physical recovery of Burma was an essential component of his strategy. First, he couldn't be sure for how long the Hump airlift (the remarkable aerial lifeline to Chungking) would survive all the other pressures of war, and in any case the airlift couldn't provide the quantity of war materiel the road was able to deliver. The recovery of the road (from Rangoon to Lashio and Bhamo) – or its rebuilding from India – would reduce this risk. Second, the physical recovery of the country would test the commitment of Britain to helping China, something about which Chiang Kai-shek was never entirely confident. By keeping relentless pressure on Britain to commit to a land invasion of Burma – even when such a thing was physically impossible due to lack of adequate troops or resources – though irritating to the British, was part of Chiang Kai-shek's strategy to keep Britain focussed on its Grand Strategic promise to America to continue its support to China.

Allied strategy in Burma since the withdrawal of the Burma Army to India and China in May 1942 and the capture of Burma by the victorious Japanese was to keep China in the war. Chiang Kai-shek's 30 divisions were holding large numbers of the Imperial Japanese Army at bay, men that could otherwise be used to counter the American advance across the Pacific and turn back the Japanese occupation of South-East Asia. A key plank of Allied Grand Strategy was, therefore, sustaining the Chinese will – as well as its physical wherewithal – to continue fighting. To do this the Burma Road, the Burmese part of which – from Rangoon by rail to Bhamo – had fallen to the Japanese in 1942, needed to be replaced or recovered. It could be replaced for a time by air, but in the long term a physical land route was required. This could be a new one across the mountains from north-eastern India, or the recapture of the old one from Rangoon. A new route, from Lashio in India down to Myitkyina would entail a massive feat of civil engineering as well as the capture of Upper Burma. Recapturing the old Burma Road would require the reconquest of the whole of Burma. In this option of difficulties

Refloating river steamers on the Irrawaddy sunk during the 1942 Allied retreat from Burma. (Victoria State Archives)

the years 1942 and 1943 would demonstrate unequivocally two things to the Allies. First, the extraordinary American chutzpah, ingenuity and resources (both human and technical) that enabled them to begin both the Hump airlift and at the same time to bulldoze a new Burma Road across the hills from Ledo towards Myitkyina in Upper Burma. Second, the complete inability of the British, for a host of issues, many of which were logistical, to even contemplate the reconquest of Burma given the paucity of supplies available either for an overland advance into Burma from the north or for an amphibious attack directly against Akyab (the main town on the Arakanese coast) or Rangoon.

Understandably, Chiang Kai-shek wanted to see concrete action by the Allies to reopen the Burma Road. He was happy with the short-term expedient of the Hump, but he wanted the certainty and security offered by a physical road. For this reason, while waiting for the road from Ledo to be built, he placed constant pressure on Britain to launch offensive operations against Burma. The United States agreed with these sentiments. But such ideas were simply not realistic until late 1944.

There were two routes the Allies could take to reconquer Burma. The first was overland from Manipur, across the Chindwin River with an offensive against Mandalay. The second was an amphibious assault directly against Rangoon. But as the abortive offensive in Arakan demonstrated, which petered out in ignominy in May 1943, the British and Indian armies were simply not strong enough or sufficiently well trained or equipped to defeat the Japanese on land. A land offensive into Upper Burma could only take place when the armies had been retrained. Equally, armchair strategists, when looking at the prospects for a land offensive across the Chindwin, often failed to appreciate the geographical realities of campaigning in this part of the world: the logistical requirements for sustaining even a corps of three Indian divisions across the Chindwin far outstripped Allied administrative capabilities until late 1944. In short, any substantial offensive into Upper Burma that had any hope of defeating the Japanese along the Irrawaddy and of capturing Mandalay was not possible until the massive logistical challenges of operating on the far eastern edge of India had been overcome. Likewise, any hope of having the amphibious resources to launch a sustainable assault against defended Akyab or Rangoon would have to wait until other Allied priorities – in 1942 in North Africa, in 1943 in Sicily and at Salerno, and in 1944 in Normandy – had been completed, and they had freed up the scarce landing craft necessary for this type of operation.

Japanese troops of the 52nd Division surrender to the 1st/10th Gurkha Rifles, 17th Indian Division, near Pegu, 23 September 1945. (Universal Images Group via Getty Images)

It was Japanese offensive operations in India, beginning in Arakan in February 1944, and ending with their defeat and withdrawal from Manipur in July and August, which opened up for the first time the realistic possibility of Allied land operations in Upper Burma.

These battles in Arakan (the 'Admin Box' and the Mayu Range 'Tunnels'), Manipur (Imphal) and Assam (Kohima) shattered the myth of Japanese invincibility that had for over two years crippled the Allied cause. They also set the seal on the efforts to rebuild the fighting power of Fourteenth Army and offered the prospect of successful offensive operations (those in 1944 were defensive) against the Japanese in Burma. Nevertheless, despite the stunning victories at Imphal and Kohima, the chiefs of staff in both London and Washington – seemingly inured to good news emanating from this theatre of war – remained ignorant for some months not just of the scale of the Japanese defeat but also of its implications for the conduct of the war in the Far East. In truth, the door to Burma across the Chindwin was now wide open, though few outside of South-East Asia Command (SEAC) saw this beckoning opportunity. In London, General Alan Brooke was still fearful in June 1944 of a disaster in Assam. Even if the Allies were eventually successful at Imphal and Kohima, he could see no virtue in giving in to Chiang Kai-shek's siren entreaties by launching a land offensive into Burma. Recapturing the country was still key in British thinking, but the operational answer to the conundrum of what to do with Burma always, in London at least, came back to an amphibious answer. A land advance into Burma was considered by most strategists to be the hardest option, the easiest one being an amphibious assault directly against Rangoon, when the resources to do so became available (scarce assets were in heavy use in Europe and the Pacific in 1944).

Consequently, because both battle and victory at Imphal and Kohima had taken them by surprise, the Allies were slow to decide how to exploit the new strategic realities offered to them by Japanese defeat in 1944. However, in mid-1944 Lieutenant-General Bill Slim, commander of the Fourteenth Army, was convinced that an aggressive policy of pursuit into Burma to exploit these victories was not just desirable but necessary. It was during these months that Slim and his headquarters staff agitated with Eleventh Army Group and Mountbatten for permission to follow up the defeat of Lieutenant-General Renya Mutaguchi's Fifteenth Army with a pursuit across the Chindwin into Upper Burma. Slim became convinced that the only sure way of defeating the Japanese in Burma was by land, and that he would have to do it with the resources at hand. With Mutaguchi's defeat Slim realized that he now had the opportunity not just to expel the remaining elements of Fifteenth Army from India, but also to

US troops in the Hukawng Valley, November 1944, fighting to open up the road from Ledo. (Hulton-Deutsch Collection/ Corbis via Getty Images)

A Mosquito fighter-bomber preparing for a sortie from a jungle airstrip somewhere in Burma in 1945. (Victoria State Archives)

pursue the Japanese back into the heart of Burma. Indeed, were he to do this, he was convinced that bigger prizes were possible, perhaps even the seizure of Rangoon itself.

However, few of his superiors saw Slim's vision as clearly as he did. His immediate superior in Eleventh Army Group – General Sir George Giffard – certainly didn't. During May 1944 Mountbatten badgered the Combined Chiefs of Staff for a decision as to what to do next, and when they did provide orders on 3 June 1944, the issue of an overland advance into Burma was fudged. So far as Washington and London were concerned, the strategic imperative remained the continued maintenance of China. The Hump still took priority. There were to be no extra resources for an amphibious assault on Burma's seaward flank, nor indeed was there any hope of additional resources to launch a land offensive into upper Burma over and above that already available. Mountbatten was nevertheless ordered 'to press advantages against the enemy by exerting maximum effort ground and air particularly during the current monsoon season'. These orders didn't tell him to invade Burma, but they did give him carte blanche to pursue his enemy. Accordingly, on 9 June 1944 Mountbatten ordered Giffard to exploit to the Chindwin between the villages of Yuwa in the south and Tamanthi in the north after the monsoon ended in October.

Slim, however, wanted more. On 2 July he met Mountbatten and persuaded him that were Fourteenth Army to mount an offensive, it could do so with no more resources than those that would anyway be allocated to the defence of India. Furthermore, he believed that an offensive could begin as early as 1 November, once the rains had lifted (the monsoon falls each year between May and October), and the pursuit of Mutaguchi's stragglers could be turned into an advance into Upper and Central Burma. But while Mountbatten was personally persuaded that a successful offensive could be mounted, at least to Shwebo or even Mandalay, Giffard was more cautious, sharing neither Mountbatten's nor Slim's optimism. He argued that it would not be possible to mount a predominantly land-based offensive across the Chindwin, nor indeed to do this during the monsoon.

Indian troops en route towards Toungoo following the battle of Meiktila, March 1945. (Victoria State Archives)

Giffard saw the victory at Imphal and Kohima more as a relief – that Fourteenth Army had not been defeated – rather than as an indication of the inherent frailties the operation had demonstrated in Japanese warfighting which could therefore be exploited to Allied advantage. Mountbatten, who had already determined to remove him, ignored Giffard's advice.

Keen to engage London on the possibility of recapturing Burma, on 23 July 1944 Mountbatten submitted two plans for approval. One had been requested by London, and the other had not. The first, Operation *Capital*, was drawn up by Slim's HQ Fourteenth Army and reflected both Mountbatten's and Slim's views of the potential for following up the retreating Fifteenth Army into Upper Burma, there to engage the Japanese armies in the region of Mandalay, linking up with Lieutenant-General Joe Stilwell's Northern Combat Area Command (NCAC) troops coming down from the north from Myitkyina, the capture of which was confidently expected soon. The second, Operation *Dracula*, requested by an amphibious-obsessed London, entailed a seaborne assault on Rangoon in early 1945 followed by an advance north to Mandalay to meet up with the Allied forces, only moving south once the capital was safely in Allied hands. London's reaction to Operation *Capital* was one of hesitation. Unaware of the spectacular success of the campaign in Manipur and Assam, few were willing to commit to the prospect of waging an offensive in a country which held so many bitter memories and which would self-evidently consume vast quantities of scarce resources. Unsurprisingly, the chiefs of staff were taken by Operation *Dracula*, as it meant not having to wage an expensive land campaign from the north, although it demanded additional forces to those already available, specifically naval forces, a further two infantry divisions and a parachute brigade, as well as large numbers of transport aircraft and gliders. They concluded that, while Slim's forces must on all accounts remain on the offensive, Fourteenth Army was to limit itself to holding operations until such time as Operation *Dracula* could be launched at Rangoon.

The Americans preferred Operation *Capital*, as it offered the greatest opportunity for opening up northern Burma, but they were prepared to consider *Dracula* if the situation in Europe allowed the transfer to the Far East of the required amphibious resources once the need for them in the invasion of France had passed. Despite this preference for *Dracula*, Slim believed that he could mount a successful offensive into Upper Burma with the resources he had to hand. It would be unfortunate if the chiefs of staff's uninformed pessimism (in his view) halted operations in Burma in favour of the supposedly easier option to land forces directly on Rangoon's doorstep from the sea. Slim knew that a strategic reprioritization to allow an amphibious assault on the south-eastern seaboard of Burma on the *Dracula* model, especially at a time when Allied eyes were firmly fixed on Europe, was highly unlikely. Despite its obvious disadvantages (mounting a two-corps offensive over nearly 1,000 miles of impossible terrain and across two of the world's largest rivers), Slim was convinced that the only certain way of defeating the Japanese in Burma was by land, and that Fourteenth Army – with its tail up following the victories in Arakan, Kohima and Imphal – had the best chance to achieve something that London and Delhi were not even contemplating.

Furthermore, Slim believed firmly that if he didn't make the running in preparing a plan to defeat the Japanese in Burma, no one would, and a great opportunity decisively to defeat the whole of the Japanese war machine in Burma would thus be squandered. The difficulty in the aftermath of Imphal lay in bringing this vision to fruition, in the face of the animosity in London

A 25-pdr field gun and jeep of XV Corps being transported on a pontoon raft down the Kalapanzin River from Buthidaung, Arakan, January 1945. (Keystone-France/Gamma-Rapho via Getty Images)

and Washington to such proposals and the instructions he had already received merely to pursue Fifteenth Army to the Chindwin. Yet Slim's clear vision throughout 1944 was undoubtedly not just to destroy Mutaguchi's army, but to launch an offensive into Burma that would succeed in driving the Japanese into the sea. The story of the reconquest of Burma in 1945 is one of Slim's determination, perseverance and bold planning, together with the ability of Fourteenth Army to pull it off.

In the second half of 1944 Slim succeeded in weaving his own strategic ambitions into the limited orders he received from Giffard to allow the momentum of chasing the defeated Mutaguchi to translate itself into a seamless offensive into Burma. It seems clear that Mountbatten and Giffard, as well as the chiefs of staff in London, accepted the success of Slim's successive offensives in Burma not just because they worked, but because they had nothing to offer as alternatives.

By September 1944 Mountbatten managed to secure from the Octagon Conference, meeting in Quebec, an extension of the earlier mandate. On 16 September he was given authority to capture all of Burma 'at the earliest date', provided that such operations did not prejudice the security of the air supply route to China, the grand strategic imperative to supply China reasserting itself. Both *Capital* and *Dracula* were approved – *Capital* to start immediately and *Dracula* to take place, hopefully, before the onset of the next monsoon in Burma in May 1945. One of the advantages of *Capital* was the chance to threaten the lines of supply of the Japanese forces facing Stilwell and the NCAC, the original purpose of Operation *Thursday*, the great Chindit expedition in the 'Railway Corridor' between Indaw and Mogaung. Mountbatten's two operations, following authorization at Quebec, were therefore:

One of the Brahmaputra ferries, part of the extraordinary Allied lines of communication between Calcutta, India and the front line in Burma. (Victoria State Archives)

Men of the Royal Scots pose for a photograph with a Japanese flag after clearing the enemy from Payan, near Shwebo, January 1945. (Imperial War Museums via Getty Images)

1. To initiate *Capital*, by capturing Kalewa and Kalemyo on the Chindwin. Fourteenth Army was to cross the Chindwin and clear the enemy from the Shwebo Plain across to the Irrawaddy, while NCAC forces (including the British 36th Division, which was landed in Myitkyina to take over the task begun by the Chindits) were to advance south to Lashio. Fourteenth Army was to advance to liberate the whole of Upper Burma to the area of Mandalay, joining up with the NCAC at Maymyo.

2. To undertake a land offensive in Arakan (Operation *Romulus*) and the capture of Akyab (Operation *Talon*). This would provide the much-needed airfield at Akyab, and release two divisions otherwise tied up in Arakan for subsequent operations in Central and Southern Burma.

Giffard had long before (on 24 July), ordered Slim to initiate planning for Operation *Capital* on the basis that, should it be sanctioned, the offensive could be put into effect in December. On the very day he received these orders, Slim was able to tell Giffard that these plans were already underway: indeed, an advance could start on 15 November, utilizing air transport to resupply forward units. To enable him to concentrate solely on this task, Giffard relieved Slim of responsibility for both Arakan (Christison's XV Corps now reported directly to Giffard at Eleventh Army Group) and the vast line of communication into Assam and Manipur for which he had been, until then, responsible. Only a month later, however, it was clear that the war in Europe would not end quickly enough to release troops and amphibious equipment for *Dracula* to take place in May 1945, and it was postponed until after the monsoon, in late 1945.

CHRONOLOGY

1944

22 June   The siege of Imphal is raised when advance units of 2nd Division link with 5th Indian Division at Milestone 107 on the Imphal to Kohima road. Operation *U-Go* collapses, the remaining Japanese withdrawing back across the Chindwin into Burma.

3 August   Myitkyina town is captured by troops of the Northern Combat Area Command (NCAC).

4 August   British 2nd Division captures Tamu.

4 November   5th Indian Division captures Kennedy Peak south of Tiddim.

5 November   Fort White, just south of Tiddim, is captured.

12 December   Operation *Romulus* is begun in Arakan by XV Corps.

1945

3 January   British commandos and an Indian brigade land on Akyab Island.

XXXIII Corps captures Yeo in its advance to the Irrawaddy.

10 January   IV Corps – Gangaw is captured.

XXXIII Corps – 19th Indian Division takes bridgeheads over the Irrawaddy north of Mandalay, at Kyaukmyang and Thabeikkyin.

XV Corps – landings by British commandos near Myebon between Akyab and Ramree.

21 January   XV Corps – landings on Ramree Island by British 4th and 71st Indian brigades.

XXXIII Corps – 20th Indian Division captures Monywa.

23 January   20th Indian Division captures Myinmu on the Irrawaddy.

26 January   XV Corps – landings on Cheduba Island, south of Ramree. The 81st African Division takes Myohaung.

IV Corps – 7th Indian Division captures Pauk.

27 January   NCAC troops meet up with Chinese troops from Yunnan, and begin to advance south towards Mandalay.

9 February   26th Indian Division completes the capture of Ramree Island.

12 February   XXXIII Corps – 20th Indian Division reaches the Irrawaddy at Myinmu.

IV Corps reaches the Irrawaddy at Myitche and Seikpyu.

NCAC fights near the Shweli River in its advance south.

13 February	20th Indian Division makes and successfully holds a bridgehead over the Irrawaddy at Myinmu, threatening Mandalay.
14 February	IV Corps – 17th Indian Division establishes a bridgehead over the Irrawaddy at Nyaungu.
	XXXIII Corps – 19th Indian Division captures Singu.
17 February	XV Corps – successful landings at Ruya, 40 miles south-east of Myebon.
	XXXIII Corps – heavy fighting along the Irrawaddy and Shweli rivers.
21 February	IV Corps – 17th Indian Division and supporting tank units begin to break out of the bridgehead at Nyaungu and advance towards Meiktila.
	XXXIII Corps – British 2nd Division crosses the Irrawaddy near Ngazun.
	NCAC – British 36th Division take Myitson on the Shweli River.
24 February	17th Indian Division captures Taungtha.
26 February	17th Indian Division captures Mablaing and the Thabutong airfield.
28 February	IV Corps attacks Meiktila.
3 March	IV Corps captures Meiktila.
5 March	Japanese counter-attacks begin against IV Corps at Meiktila, recapturing Taungtha and cutting off 17th Indian Division.
6 March	Chinese New First Army captures Lashio.
8 March	XXXIII Corps – both British 2nd and 20th Indian divisions begin to break out of the bridgeheads over the Irrawaddy to the west of Mandalay.
9 March	19th Indian Division reaches Mandalay.
11 March	NCAC – British 36th Division captures Mongmit.
12 March	20th Indian Division captures Myotha.
14 March	62nd Indian Brigade captures Maymyo.
17 March	NCAC – Chinese New Sixth Army takes Hswipaw on the Burma Road, 50 miles south-west of Lashio.
	XXXIII Corps – 2nd Division captures Ava.
19 March	NCAC – British 36th Division captures Mogok.
	XXXIII Corps – 19th Indian Division captures Mandalay.
23 March	XXXIII Corps – 20th Indian Division races south and captures Wundwin.
28 March	Japanese relinquish efforts to recapture Meiktila. The battle is over.

30 March	XXXIII Corps – 20th Indian Division captures Kyaukse.
31 March	NCAC – 36th Division and Chinese Sixth Army take Kyaukme.
10 April	IV Corps captures Thazi.
12 April	IV Corps advances down the Sittang Valley towards Toungoo.
	7th Indian Division captures Kyaukpaduang.
15 April	20th Indian Division captures Taungdwingyi.
16 April	XV Corps – Taungup is captured.
19 April	IV Corps – 5th Indian Division captures Pyinmana.
	XXXIII Corps captures Mount Popa area and Chauk and 20th Indian Division captures Magwe.
21 April	IV Corps advances quickly on Toungoo.
	XXXIII Corps captures Yenangyaung.
22 April	5th Indian Division captures Toungoo.
25 April	5th Indian Division advances south, capturing Perwegen.
29 April	XXXIII Corps captures Allamnyo.
	IV Corps – 17th Indian Division takes the lead from 5th Indian Division, captures Nyaunglebim and attacks Payagyi.
1 May	The 17th Indian Division approaches Pegu.
	Monsoon rains begin.
2 May	Operation *Dracula* begins, with 26th Indian Division landing unopposed.
3 May	26th Indian Division captures Rangoon.
	XXXIII Corps captures Prome, on the Irrawaddy.
6 May	26th Indian Division meets up with units of IV Corps at Hlegu.
3–7 July	First Battle of the Sittang Bend, as the Japanese Thirty-Third Army attempts to break out into Tenasserim.
15 July	Second Battle of the Sittang Bend, as the Japanese Twenty-Eighth Army begins its attempt to break out.
21–29 July	Third Battle of the Sittang Bend.
15 August	Emperor Hirohito announces the Japanese surrender in Tokyo.
13 September	Last units of the Japanese Burma Area Army surrender.

OPPOSING COMMANDERS

JAPANESE

The commander-in-chief of the Burma Area Army was 66-year-old **General Heitaro Kimura**. Arriving from Tokyo in September 1944 via a briefing in Saigon, to replace General Kawabe, he was given the task of defending Burma against the newly resurgent Allies, who were flush with victory at Imphal and Kohima and knocking insistently at Burma's western and northern doors. Highly regarded in Tokyo, where he had been Vice Minister for War, Kimura was a career artilleryman who had served as a military attaché in Germany in the 1920s and as one of the Japanese military representatives at the London Disarmament Conference between 1929 and 1930. From 1935 he sat at the heart of Japanese military planning in its expanding military ambitions in China, and between 1939 and 1940 commanded 32nd Division in China before serving as the chief of staff to the Kwantung Army in Manchukuo.

General Heitaro Kimura. (Wikipaedia Commons)

He was therefore deeply imbued with Japanese aspirations to create a martial hegemony for Japan in East and South-East Asia. He returned to Tokyo as a lieutenant-general in April 1941 where he became Vice Minister of War and a member of the Planning Board. As such he played a significant role in planning offensive operations across South-East Asia in December 1941.

A man steeped in the military ambitions of the era, he was considered the best person, with his knowledge of Britain and his command experience, to rescue Japan's irons from the fire in Burma in late 1944.

Kimura reported to **Field Marshal Count Hisaichi Terauchi**, commander of the Southern Army, based in Saigon. Kimura had three armies in Burma: the Fifteenth, Twenty-Eighth and Thirty-Third (a Japanese army equated in size to a British/Indian corps).

The command of Fifteenth Army was given to **Major-General Shihachi Katamura** on 30 August with the departure of General Renya Mutaguchi following the catastrophic failure of Operation

U-Go. Katamura was a long-serving divisional commander, known to be steady and dependable. He had commanded 54th Division since August 1941, arriving in Burma in January 1944, serving first in Twenty-Eighth Army in Arakan. Fifteenth Army's role was to defend north-western Burma along and above the Irrawaddy.

Twenty-Eighth Army was commanded by **Major-General Shozo Sakurai**. He was a well-liked and vastly experienced divisional commander, commanding 22nd Division in China in 1938–39 prior to becoming Chief of Staff of Thirteenth Army in China. He had then commanded 33rd Division in General Shojiro Iida's victorious Fifteenth Army during the invasion of Burma in early 1942. He very nearly captured the entire command structure of Burma Army (including General Sir Harold Alexander) during the battle for Rangoon in March 1942, before pushing the retreating Burma Corps north. His division was then responsible for the defence of Arakan, successfully pushing back a poorly executed British offensive between late 1942 and May 1943. After spending part of 1943 in a staff appointment in Tokyo, he returned to take command of the newly constituted Twenty-Eighth Army in January 1944. He was not responsible for the planning and execution of the Japanese offensive against British and Indian forces in northern Arakan in February 1944 (Operation *Ha-Go*), a strategic feint to draw off British reserves from the main Japanese effort against Manipur and Assam (Operation *U-Go*).[1] The attack involved in all about 7,500 experienced troops, but it failed miserably, defeated by improved British and Indian tactics and fighting confidence, as well as by a massive Allied advantage in air supply which allowed their troops to stay put when surrounded, confident that plentiful combat supplies could be brought to them by air. By 22 February 1944 Sakurai's army had been defeated and was in retreat. Interestingly, Sakurai seemed to display little of the martial bombast that characterized his peers. When he reluctantly authorized the construction of a victory monument in Burma following the 1942 invasion (believing correctly that it was premature), he insisted that a memorial for the British and Indian fallen was erected as well.

Thirty-Third Army, established in April 1944 to resist Allied encroachment into Upper Burma, was commanded by **Major-General Masaki Honda**. Another divisional commander who had cut his teeth in China, he was vice chief of staff of the China Expeditionary Army in 1939 and commander of 8th Division in Manchuria in 1941. He took command of Twentieth Army in Manchuria in 1943 before being sent to Burma to take command of Thirty-Third Army when it was raised in April 1944. A cool tactician, and well liked by his men, he had an unusual proclivity for telling obscene stories of such crudity that even his soldiers were left aghast on the hearing of them.

Kimura and his three army commanders – Katamura, Sakurai and Honda – all newly appointed to their posts, at least demonstrated that the Japanese had learned one thing from the command chaos that had reigned the previous year in **Lieutenant-General Renya Mutaguchi's** Fifteenth Army. The destructive relationship between Mutaguchi and his three divisional commanders – **lieutenant-generals Motoso Yanagida, Masafumi**

---

1 It was planned by General Tadashi Hanaya, the hard-bitten commander of 55th Division and led – confusingly – by Major-General Tokutaro Sakurai, his infantry commander.

Yamauchi and **Kotoku Sato** – which had had such a deleterious effect on the conduct of operations against Imphal and Kohima, was not to be repeated in 1945.

ALLIED

The Supreme Allied Commander SEAC from late 1943 was **Admiral Lord Louis Mountbatten**. A reorganization of land forces a year later on 12 November 1944 brought all Allied land forces into a single command, Allied Land Forces South-East Asia (ALFSEA), commanded by **General Sir Oliver Leese**, who until this time had commanded the British Eighth Army in Italy. Mountbatten's second-in-command was the American **Lieutenant-General Raymond Wheeler** who replaced the departing **Lieutenant-General Joseph Stilwell**.

ALFSEA comprised 20 combat divisions, in Fourteenth Army, XV Corps, and the NCAC (which included the British 36th Division), together with the Line of Communication Command and Ceylon Army Command. The

General Sir Oliver Leese addresses his troops. (Victoria State Archives)

The crew of a 40mm Bofors anti-aircraft gun of 11th East African Division watch as an RAF Dakota drops supplies on the western side of the Chindwin River, between 8 and 11 December 1944. (Victoria State Archives)

widespread reorganization at the time included abolishing the Troop Carrier Command and creating a single, joint army/air supply organization – Combat Cargo Task Force – at Comilla, with two separate components. The army ran the Combined Army Air Transport Organization, which organized the entirety of Fourteenth Army and XV Corps' aerial logistic requirements, and the RAF ran the Combat Cargo Task Force, which ensured that sufficient aircraft were available to meet the demands of the army. This requirement was substantial. In the period between December 1944 and May 1945, an average of 60,000 tons of supplies were being delivered by airlift each month, and in March a record of 78,250 tons, together with 27,000 military passengers: a peak day saw 4,000 tons being airlifted for troops in Arakan and Central Burma.

The previous HQ, 3rd Tactical Air Force was disbanded, and 221st and 224th groups were placed directly under Eastern Air Command, reflecting a more streamlined and joint operation that removed, as far as was possible, the distinctions between army and air force when meeting the needs of the fighting formations on the ground.

From the outset Leese had an unhappy relationship with Slim. Leese wanted to exercise command, as was his right; Slim, however, knew what he wanted to achieve, and how to do so. As the author of Operation *Capital*, he didn't

Air Vice Marshal S.F. Vincent, Air Officer Commander-in-Chief of No. 221 Group RAF (centre), watches Hawker Hurricanes take off from Sadaung on a strafing operation during the advance on Mandalay, with Lieutenant-General Bill Slim, commander of Fourteenth Army (right), and Group Captain D.O. Finlay, Commanding Officer of No. 906 Wing RAF (left). (Imperial War Museum)

want to be told what to do, and in this respect proved to be a difficult subordinate. Leese, for his part, arrived with a critical attitude, perhaps with echoes of the 1942 and 1943 failures still in his ear. He expected to have to remedy tactical deficiencies in his commanders, and 'grip' operations to ensure success as Fourteenth Army launched itself into Upper and Central Burma, and as XV Corps tried for the third time to make headway in Arakan. On first impressions he considered that Slim was 'sound in his tactics', but Leese didn't consider the victory at Imphal and Kohima to be on a par with those achieved in North Africa and Italy.

Major-General David 'Punch' Cowan, GOC 17th Indian Division (left) in conversation with Lieutenant-General Bill Slim (right). (Public domain)

For operations in Burma, XV Corps in Arakan under the command of **Lieutenant-General Sir Philip Christison** was split from the remainder of Fourteenth Army, which remained under the command of the victor of Imphal and Kohima, **Lieutenant-General Bill Slim.** Responsibility for the NCAC was transferred from Lieutenant-General Joseph Stilwell to **General Dan Sultan,** who was simultaneously commander of the US Burma-India Theater.[2]

Lieutenant-General Bill Slim was promoted to temporary command of the Eastern Army in August 1943 at a time when British fortunes in the Far East were at their lowest ebb (his predecessor had been sacked). Tough, wise and accessible to all, he was the epitome of the great commander. Against the most formidable of obstacles, he helped to transform Allied fortunes in Burma such that profound defeat in 1942 was turned into overwhelming and comprehensive victory in 1945.

Slim's great success lay in understanding what it would take to defeat the Japanese in battle, and what he needed to do to his army to achieve this objective, which in 1943 seemed impossibly distant. In addition to developing a strategy for defeating Mutaguchi's offensive in 1944, Slim worked from first principles in 1943 to transform the morale and motivation of his men: Indian and Gurkha (predominately), African and British. He did this so spectacularly that by the end of the desperate battles against the Japanese in 1944 Slim had become 'Uncle Bill', a sobriquet soon in universal currency in Fourteenth Army, and which was to remain with him for the rest of his life.

For the offensive into Burma in late 1944, Fourteenth Army comprised two corps: IV and XXXIII. IV Corps was commanded by the newly promoted **Lieutenant-General Frank Messervy,** fresh from his victories in Arakan as commander of 7th Indian Division. **Lieutenant-General Montagu Stopford** commanded XXXIII Corps, which had been responsible for fighting and winning the Battle of Kohima.

---

2   Unlike Stilwell's China-Burma-India (CBI) theatre, Sultan's new command did not include China.

OPPOSING FORCES

JAPANESE

By late 1944 the Japanese armies in Burma had met their match in the British and Indian armies that they faced in Arakan, Manipur and Assam during that year. The Japanese Twenty-Eighth Army offensive in Arakan (*Ha-Go*) had been thrown back in ignominy, as had Fifteenth Army under Mutaguchi at Imphal and Kohima (*U-Go*). In the north, Lieutenant-General Joe Stilwell's NCAC had captured Myitkyina and for the first time a coordinated threat to the Japanese in Burma offered itself.

But the Japanese retained an extraordinary ability to keep on fighting, even in defeat. When Slim looked at the odds against him in late 1944 – especially those in Upper Burma – his two corps were still outnumbered. Kimura's forces, chastened but far from beaten, amounted to five and a half divisions, an independent mixed brigade, a tank regiment, nearly 40,000 line of communication troops, two Indian National Army (INA) divisions and troops of General Aung San's Burma Defence Army (BDA).

Despite their defeats in 1944, the Japanese soldier continued to exhibit remarkable fighting qualities. The basis of his fighting ability was the survival through long years of war of the bushido code, which defined the life, purpose, motivations and ultimately the death of the Japanese soldier. Loyalty to the emperor was an inviolable spiritual and moral duty for all soldiers. The ultimate purpose of a samurai was not merely obedience, but death. Disobedience, disloyalty or failure was inconceivable. All professional soldiers of the time included in their daily routine obeisance to the emperor, through a ritual and energetic '*Banzai!*' ('May the Emperor live for 10,000 years!'), bowing in prayer in the direction of Tokyo. The bushido code entailed a commitment – philosophical, intellectual, intensely practical and even religious – to a set of obligations that lead inevitably to death in the service of a heroic ideal. These obligations were enshrined by Prime Minister Hideki Tojo in the 'Soldier Code' issued in 1941, and obliged the true samurai to die in the service of his country and emperor, rather than surrender, which was despised as the route of the coward and scoundrel. This, in part, explains much of the animosity displayed by Japanese troops to surrendered enemy personnel.

Tough, frugal and determined, the Japanese were far better prepared and equipped in 1941 and 1942 for a savage jungle-based war than the British and Indian soldiers who opposed them. Japanese tactics copied those of the European blitzkrieg ideal, designed above all to achieve shock and paralysis in their enemy. In this they proved to be resoundingly successful. The seemingly inaccessible jungle, a place of fear for many British and Imperial troops, was used by the Japanese extensively for movement. Commanders sought routinely to disrupt and confuse their enemy. Roads and headquarters were attacked in order to paralyze British command and control arrangements, overload commanders and cause confusion among the troops. The Japanese had a particular penchant for emerging from the jungle far to the rear of a main position and setting up roadblocks on the all-important lines of communication upon which the British relied for movement and supplies. By infiltrating behind and through British defensive positions, they would make the defenders believe that they were cut off with no hope of escape, and by moving quickly through thick jungle to appear far behind the 'front line' they would induce panic. They moved quickly and lightly, unencumbered with the scales of transport and materiel of war that characterized the British. At the outset of the war the Japanese were amazed at the ease with which they could psychologically dominate their opponents, sometimes achieving their objectives without having to do much fighting.

During their relentless advance through Burma in the first five months of 1942 and during the abortive British offensive in Arakan the following year, the Japanese forced the British to play to their tune. The Japanese method of war, their single-minded determination to win, together with their savagery and wanton disregard for life, their own or their enemy's, came as a brutal shock to the European military tradition and its deeply rooted codes of military conduct and chivalry that still held sway in the British and Indian armies. To the ordinary fighting man – but particularly the Indian and British soldier (the Gurkha was not similarly affected) – the Japanese soldier quickly gained fame as a fearsome fighting beast for which none of their training had prepared them. Their ferocity in the offensive (such as the invasion of Burma in 1942) and their remarkable staying power when

A column of Japanese POWs heads to a holding camp in Burma following the surrender of Japan on 15 August 1945. (Victoria State Archives)

A section of three Spitfire Mark VIIIs of No. 136 Squadron flies over other aircraft parked on an airfield in northern Burma in early 1945. By late 1944, the Allies had secured air superiority over Burma, which allowed for the comprehensive use of air transport to support the forward deployment of ground forces. (Victoria State Archives)

on the defensive (such as in Arakan in 1943) gave the Japanese a dramatic psychological advantage over Indian and British troops and allowed them to dominate the battlefield, creating an aura of invincibility about the Japanese 'superman' that was to take two years for the British to erase.

However, despite these stunning early successes, the Imperial Japanese Army remained remarkably backward in adopting modern methods and equipment. Its supply arrangements were simplistic, its artillery provision was weak and by 1944 its air support virtually non-existent. In the three months between April and June 1944 during the battles for Imphal and Kohima the total number of Allied air sorties including transport flights directly in support of the troops engaged in battle exceeded 30,000. In contrast, limited aircraft numbers meant that the Japanese could mount a mere 1,750 sorties over the battlefields during this time, and by the end of July only 49 aircraft remained in the Japanese inventory. A significant Japanese weakness lay in the fact that most of their aircraft were fighters: they possessed no transport capability and only a tiny bomber force that was frittered away early in the fighting. One of Tokyo's worst miscalculations in 1944 was failing to anticipate the combined strength of Allied air forces, without which the defence of India would not have been possible. Japanese commanders saw the invasion of India as an exercise in ground warfare, and in their assessments (if, indeed, they ever made them) of Allied air power they failed grievously to appreciate this war-winning capability enjoyed by their enemy, and their own dramatic weakness.

Indeed, the Japanese were ignorant in 1944 of the dramatic improvements made in Allied training, tactics, leadership and morale since the early years of the fighting and the end of the failed offensive in Arakan in 1943. This was one of the reasons for the collapse of an offensive the Tokyo propagandists, egged on by the exiled Bengali nationalist Subhas Chandra Bose, called 'The March on Delhi'. In almost every respect, apart from their renowned martial chutzpah, the Japanese were unprepared for the cauldron of battle into which they so enthusiastically threw themselves, thinking that this was an easy re-run of the quick victories they had enjoyed against unprepared opponents in 1941 and 1942. Their logistical plans were wildly optimistic. Equally, the dynamism of Japanese leadership which secured such dramatic successes in 1942 had waned significantly by 1944 and left them less able to cope with a very different battlefield and a vastly different enemy from that which they had encountered in 1941 and 1942.

Now, in late 1944, the Japanese had been thrown onto their back foot, and faced the defence of occupied Burma. For the first time their defensive strategies would be tested to the full.

The Japanese had in Burma ten divisions together with a single, severely depleted, air division. As at mid-November 1944 General Kimura had under his command the units listed in the below order of battle.

JAPANESE ORDER OF BATTLE, MID-NOVEMBER 1944

FIFTEENTH ARMY

Lieutenant-General Renya Mutaguchi; from 30 August 1944,
Lieutenant-General Shihachi Katamura
Tasked with defending the Irrawaddy.

15th Division (Lieutenant-General Masafumi Yamauchi; from January 1945, Major-General Seiei Yamamoto)
Strength: about 4,500 men
51st Infantry Regiment
60th Infantry Regiment
67th Infantry Regiment
21st Field Artillery Regiment

31st Division (Lieutenant-General Kotoku Sato; from 7 July 1944 after Kohima, Major-General Tsuchitato Kawada)
Strength: about 7,000 men
58th Infantry Regiment
124th Infantry Regiment
138th Infantry Regiment
31st Mountain Artillery Regiment
1st/21st Field Artillery Battalion (seconded from 15th Division)
(Elements of) 3rd Heavy Artillery Regiment
3rd Anti-Tank Battery
31st Engineer Regiment
20th Independent Engineer Regiment

33rd Division (Lieutenant-General Nobuo Tanaka)
Strength: about 5,400 men
213th Infantry Regiment
214th Infantry Regiment
215th Infantry Regiment
33rd Mountain Artillery Regiment
(Elements of) 18th Heavy Field Artillery Regiment
3rd/2nd Field Artillery Battalion
33rd Engineer Regiment
4th Independent Engineer Regiment

53rd Division (Lieutenant-General Yoshihide Hayashi, transferred from Thirty-Third Army in late 1944)
Strength: about 4,500 men
119th Infantry Regiment
128th Infantry Regiment
151st Infantry Regiment
53rd Field Artillery Regiment (less 3rd/53rd Field Artillery Battalion, not in Burma)

TWENTY-EIGHTH ARMY

Lieutenant-General Shozo Sakurai
In Arakan.

54th Division (Lieutenant-General Shigesaburo Miyazaki)
111th Infantry Regiment
121st Infantry Regiment
154th Infantry Regiment
54th Field Artillery Regiment
54th Engineer Regiment

55th Division (Lieutenant-General Tadashi Hanaya)
112th Infantry Regiment
143rd Infantry Regiment
144th Infantry Regiment
55th Mountain Artillery Regiment
55th Engineer Regiment

72nd Independent Mixed Brigade (Major-General Tsunoru Yamamoto)[3]
187th Infantry Battalion
188th Infantry Battalion

542nd Infantry Battalion
543rd Infantry Battalion
72nd Brigade Artillery Unit
72nd Brigade Engineer Unit

THIRTY-THIRD ARMY

Lieutenant-General Masaki Honda
In Bhamo.

18th Division (Lieutenant-General Shinichi Tanaka)[4]
55th Infantry Regiment
56th Infantry Regiment
114th Infantry Regiment
18th Mountain Artillery Regiment
12th Engineer Regiment

56th Division (Lieutenant-General Yuzo Matsuyama)
113th Infantry Regiment
146th Infantry Regiment
148th Infantry Regiment
56th Field Artillery Regiment
56th Engineer Regiment

AREA ARMY RESERVE

2nd Division (Lieutenant-General Keishin Managi)[5]
4th Infantry Regiment
16th Infantry Regiment
29th Infantry Regiment
2nd Field Artillery Regiment
2nd Engineer Regiment

49th Division (Lieutenant-General Saburo Takehara)
106th Infantry Regiment
153rd Infantry Regiment
168th Infantry Regiment
49th Mountain Artillery Regiment
49th Engineer Regiment

24th Independent Mixed Brigade (Lieutenant-General Yoshihide Hayashi)[6]
138th Infantry Battalion
139th Infantry Battalion
140th Infantry Battalion
141st Infantry Battalion
24th Brigade Artillery Unit
24th Brigade Engineer Unit

5th Air Division[7]
50th Air Regiment (twenty fighters)
64th Air Regiment (twenty fighters)
13th Air Regiment (ten fighters)[8]
8th Air Regiment (thirteen light bombers)
81st Air Regiment (fifteen reconnaissance aircraft)
204th Air Regiment (two fighters)[9]

Burma National Army (Major-General Aung San) and remnants of the Indian National Army
Seven battalions

---

3   Yamamoto was previously the infantry group commander of 33rd Division during Operation *U-Go*.

4   Largely destroyed in the fighting up to September 1944. Its commander Shinichi Tanaka became chief of staff of the Burma Area Army.
5   Managi was transferred in late 1944.
6   Until Hayashi was promoted to command 53rd Division in late 1944.
7   Moved to French Indo-China in February 1945.
8   From January 1945.
9   From December 1944.

ALLIED

Pushed out of Burma in May 1942, following a 1,000-mile retreat back to India, the British had been humiliated by Japanese boldness, professionalism and panache. The limited offensive into Burma along the Arakan coast in May 1943 had ended in dismal failure, demonstrating once again that at the time British and Indian troops remained ill matched against the hardy, aggressive, triumphant Japanese.

By early 1944, however, much had changed in the British and Indian armies, and the Japanese now found themselves facing an enemy that was immeasurably better prepared, equipped, trained and led than it had been only eight months before. Lieutenant-General Bill Slim was convinced that he could transform the fortunes of his troops, despite the many gainsayers who loudly claimed the Japanese to be unbeatable. His basic prescription – in which he was supported wholeheartedly by a new raft of divisional commanders such as Douglas Gracey (20th Indian Division), Ouvry Roberts (23rd Indian Division) and Frank Messervy (17th Indian Division) among others – was rigorous and realistic training for all troops. Imaginative and demanding training was instituted, both for the individual soldier and his unit – section, platoon, company and battalion. Training in simulated battlefield conditions enabled soldiers to cope with the demands of fighting a tenacious enemy in the harsh physical environment of both mountain and jungle. He was certain that if men were adequately prepared to overcome these challenges, if they were helped to do so by better medical care (especially to prevent the mass casualties caused in 1942 and 1943 by malaria) and if the lines of communication supplying the troops in forward areas with food, fuel and ammunition were made more secure – by using air supply rather than relying on tracks and roads – morale would improve, and with it the troops' certainty that they could defeat the Japanese in battle.

Despite the demands posed by the torrential monsoon rains that fell each year between May and October, physical toughening, weapon training and long cross-country marches – on foot and with mules – carried out over

Transport of the 5th Indian Division struggling through mud on the Tiddim front, 1944. (Imperial War Museums via Getty Images)

hills, through jungle and across rivers became the order of the day. Live firing with rifles, machine guns and grenades in realistic conditions – often at the end of exhausting marches over huge distances in day and night, and through the dank, sun-parched jungle – was practised constantly. Exercises ranged from patrol actions by sections and platoons, ambushes up to company level to battalion attacks coordinated with artillery and aircraft. In addition, night training, field discipline and mock battles with live ammunition, mortars and artillery in all weathers became the

Slim's Fourteenth Army was polyglot. Here, Indian soldiers and men of the 81st West African Division pose together following the 81st's arrival in India for jungle training in 1942. The first African colonial troops to fight outside Africa, the 81st Division entered Burma in December 1943. (Imperial War Museums via Getty Images)

norm. Training was hard and embraced every soldier in every type of unit, including men who in earlier times in the Indian Army would have been regarded as non-combatants. It was essential, if under the strain of battle exhausted soldiers were able to conquer their fear, think clearly and shoot straight in a crisis and inspire maximum physical and mental endeavour. They needed to overcome the tremendous psychological demands entailed in fighting the Japanese, who as a matter of course ruthlessly exploited mistakes caused by inexperience or complacency. In time, this training, together with carefully choreographed engagements with the Japanese, demonstrated that the Japanese were not bogeymen, and could be beaten. Officers who did not make the grade were removed and replaced.

Units of both the British and Indian armies were taught how to cooperate with the various arms and services, and with the Royal Air Force and Indian Air Force. Signals, engineer and artillery courses blossomed, as did air-to-ground cooperation courses, infantry and tank cooperation training, parachute, air-landing and glider training, and innumerable other courses

A DUKW crosses the Irrawaddy in February 1945. (Imperial War Museum)

and instruction dealing with everything from the provision of air-dropped supplies to the proper crossing of rivers.

Fourteenth Army was well supported by air, especially by transport (largely provided by the Americans), which meant that Slim was able to move forces quickly to where they were most needed. Troops on the ground, even small numbers who found themselves on long-range patrol, or who were cut off by Japanese encirclement, could depend on rapid and accurate air drops of essential supplies – including fuel, ammunition, food and water – when required.

The dramatic battles in northern Arakan, Imphal and Kohima between February and June 1944 demonstrated the profound changes that had taken place in both the British and Indian armies since 1942, to allow these victories to occur. Now, in late 1944, these armies had their tails up. They knew that the Japanese were not invincible, and had demonstrated their mastery of the battlefield convincingly.

The primary combat elements of Fourteenth Army HQ and Army troops comprised units attached to Fourteenth Army, troops attached to each of IV Corps and XXXIII Corps, and infantry divisions and unattached brigades that were ordered and re-ordered as the operational requirement demanded.[10]

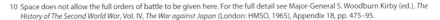

10 Space does not allow the full orders of battle to be given here. For the full detail see Major-General S. Woodburn Kirby (ed.), *The History of The Second World War*, Vol. IV, *The War against Japan* (London: HMSO, 1965), Appendix 18, pp. 475–95.

Troops of the 11th East African Division on the road to Kalewa, Burma, during the Chindwin River crossing in late 1944. (Imperial War Museum)

FOURTEENTH ARMY ORDER OF BATTLE

Lieutenant-General William Slim
Armour (armoured cars)
8th King George V's Light Cavalry
11th Cavalry
Artillery
18th Self-Propelled Field Regiment, Royal Artillery
134th Medium Regiment, Royal Artillery
52nd Heavy Anti-Aircraft Regiment, Royal Artillery
69th Light Anti-Aircraft Regiment, Royal Artillery
2nd Indian Field Regiment
2nd Indian Light Anti-Aircraft Regiment
5th Mahratta Anti-Tank Regiment
Engineers (all Indian Engineers)
4 x Works companies
2 x Bridging companies
3 x Bridging platoons
4 x Engineer battalions
4 x Field companies
Forward Airfield Engineers
    Engineer Battalion
    2 x Engineer companies
    1 x Mechanical Equipment Platoon
Infantry
1st/3rd Madras Regiment
1st Assam Rifles
3rd Assam Rifles
4th Assam Rifles
Chin Hills Battalion
25th Gurkha Rifles
Western Chin Levies
Lushai Scouts
Logistics
590th Tank Transport Company
Elephant Company, Royal Indian Army Service Corps
387th Divisional Troops Company (DUKWs)
5th Indian Field Ambulance

IV CORPS

Lieutenant-General Sir Frank Messervy
Armour
255th Indian Tank Brigade
8th Medium Regiment, Royal Artillery
1st Light Anti-Aircraft Regiment, Indian Army
67th Heavy Anti-Aircraft Regiment, Indian Army
Engineers, Signals, Infantry

XXXIII CORPS

Lieutenant-General Sir Montagu Stopford
Armour
254th Indian Tank Brigade
1st Medium Regiment, Royal Artillery
44th Light Anti-Aircraft Regiment, Royal Artillery
101st Heavy Anti-Aircraft Regiment, Royal Artillery
8th Mahratta Anti-Tank Regiment
Engineers, Signals, Infantry

INFANTRY DIVISIONS OF FOURTEENTH ARMY

British 2nd Division
3 x Field regiments, Royal Artillery
1 x Anti-Tank Regiment, Royal Artillery
3 x Field companies, Royal Engineers
Machine-Gun Battalion
4th, 5th and 6th (infantry) brigades
5th Indian Division
2 x Field regiments Royal Artillery
1 x Anti-Tank Regiment, Royal Artillery
1 x Indian Mountain Regiment

3 x Field companies, Indian Engineers
3 x Infantry battalions
9th, 123rd and 161st Indian (infantry) brigades
7th Indian Division
2 x Field regiments Royal Artillery
1 x Anti-Tank Regiment, Royal Artillery
1 x Indian Mountain Regiment
3 x Field companies, Indian Engineers
3 x Infantry battalions
33rd, 89th and 11th Indian (infantry) brigades
11th East African Division
2 x East African Field regiments
1 x East African Anti-Tank Regiment
3 x East African Field companies
2 x Infantry battalions
21st, 25th and 26th East African (infantry) brigades
17th Indian Division
1 x Field Regiment, Royal Artillery
1 x Indian Field Regiment
1 x Indian Mountain Regiment
1 x Anti-Tank Regiment, Royal Artillery
3 x Field companies, Indian Engineers
3 x Infantry battalions
48th, 63rd and 99th Indian (infantry) brigades
19th Indian Division
1 x Field Regiment, Royal Artillery
1 x Indian Field Regiment
1 x Anti-Tank Regiment, Royal Artillery
1 x Indian Mountain Regiment
3 x Field companies, Royal Engineers
3 x Infantry battalions
62nd, 64th and 98th Indian (infantry) brigades
20th Indian Division
2 x Field regiments, Royal Artillery
1 x Anti-Tank Regiment, Royal Artillery
1 x Indian Mountain Regiment
3 x Field companies, Royal Engineers
3 x Infantry battalions
32nd, 80th and 100th Indian (infantry) brigades

INDEPENDENT INFANTRY BRIGADES

268th Indian Brigade
Lushai Brigade
28th East African Brigade

XV CORPS

Lieutenant-General Sir Philip Christison
Arakan.
Armour
50th Indian Tank Brigade
6th Medium Regiment, Royal Artillery
36th Light Anti-Aircraft Regiment, Royal Artillery
8th Heavy Anti-Aircraft Regiment, Royal Artillery
8th Mahratta Anti-Tank Regiment
Engineers, Signals, Infantry
22nd East African Brigade
3 Commando Brigade

INFANTRY DIVISIONS OF XV CORPS
25th Indian Division
2 x Field regiments, Royal Artillery
1 x Anti-Tank Regiment, Royal Artillery
1 x Indian Mountain Regiment
3 x Field companies, Royal Engineers
2 x Infantry battalions
51st, 53rd and 74th Indian (infantry) brigades

26th Indian Division
1 x Field Regiment, Royal Artillery
1 x Indian Field Regiment
1 x Anti-Tank Regiment, Royal Artillery
1 x Indian Mountain Regiment
3 x Field companies, Royal Engineers
1 x Infantry Battalion
4th, 36th and 71st Indian (infantry) brigades
81st West African Division
1 x West African Anti-Tank Regiment
1 x West African Mortar Regiment
1 x West African Light Regiment
3 x West African Field companies
1 x Infantry Battalion
5th and 6th West African (infantry) brigades
82nd West African Division
1 x West African Anti-Tank Regiment
1 x West African Mortar Regiment
1 x West African Light Regiment
3 x West African Field companies
1 x Infantry Battalion
1st, 2nd and 4th West African (infantry) brigades

NORTHERN COMBAT AREA COMMAND

Lieutenant-General Dan Sultan
Mars Task Force
1 x US Field Artillery Battalion
1 x US Infantry Regiment
1 x US Cavalry Regiment
1 x Chinese Regiment
New Chinese First Army (Lieutenant-General Sun Li-jen)
New 22nd Division
New 30th Division
New 38th Division
New Chinese Sixth Army
14th Division
22nd Division
50th Division
British 36th Division
2 x Field regiments, Royal Artillery
1 x Anti-Tank Regiment, Royal Artillery
1 x Indian Mountain Regiment
2 x Field companies, Indian Engineers
1 x Field Company, Royal Engineers
2 x Bridging platoons, Indian Engineers
1 x Machine-Gun Company
British 29th, 26th Indian and 72nd Indian (infantry) brigades[11]

EASTERN AIR COMMAND,[12] 12 DECEMBER 1944

No. 221 Group RAF (Air Vice Marshal Vincent)
Imphal.
No. 906 Wing, Imphal
    One IAF Hurricane squadron
    Two RAF Hurricane squadrons
No. 907 Wing, Tamu
    One RAF Spitfire squadron
    One RAF Hurricane squadron
No. 908 Wing, Kumbhirgram
    One RAF Mosquito squadron
No. 909 Wing, Palel
    Three RAF Spitfire squadrons
    Two RAF Hurricane squadrons
No. 910 Wing, Wangjing
    Three RAF Thunderbolt squadrons
No. 224 Group RAF (Air Vice Marshal The Earl of Bandon)
Cox's Bazar.
No. 901 Wing, Chiringa

Three RAF Beaufighter squadrons
No. 902 Wing, Chittagong
    One IAF Hurricane squadron
    Two RAF Thunderbolt squadrons
    One USAAF P-38 Lightning squadron
No. 903 Wing, Comilla
    One RAF Spitfire squadron
No. 905 Wing, Chiringa
    Two RAF Thunderbolt squadrons
10th USAAF (Major General Howard Davidson)
Myitkyina.
80th Fighter Group[13]
    Three Thunderbolt squadrons
33rd Fighter Group
    Three P-38 Lightning squadrons
    One Mitchell B-25 squadron
3rd US Combat Cargo Group, Dinjan
    Four C-47 squadrons
443rd Troop Carrier Group, Ledo
    Three C-47 squadrons[14]
Combat Cargo Task Force (Brigadier-General Frederick Evans)
Comilla.
1st US Combat Cargo Group, Tulihal (Imphal)
    Four C-47 squadrons
    177th Transport Wing RAF, Comilla
        Four C-47 squadrons
    4th US Combat Cargo Group, Sylhet/Agartala
        Four C-47 squadrons
    1st US Air Commando Group, Comilla/Ledo
        One C-47 squadron
Strategic Air Force, Calcutta
No. 231 Group RAF
    No. 175 Wing
        One B-24 Liberator squadron
    No. 184 Wing
        Two B-24 Liberator squadrons
    No. 185 Wing
        Three B-24 Liberator squadrons
    No. 7 Bombardment Group USAAF
        Four B-24 Liberator squadrons
    No. 12 Bombardment Group USAAF
        Four B-25 Mitchell squadrons

---

11 72nd Indian Brigade comprised three British infantry battalions.
12 Part of Air Command, South-East Asia.

13 A USAAF group was the same size as an RAF wing.
14 US troop carrier squadrons had 16 aircraft; RAF squadrons had 25 aircraft each.

OPPOSING PLANS

By July 1944 Slim knew that the Japanese had received a defeat the like of which would make it difficult for them to recover quickly. If he could engineer a second defeat for the Japanese in Upper Burma – by sending his army in pursuit across the Chindwin River – it would seriously weaken the Japanese defensive potential in Lower Burma, greatly enabling the success of an overland thrust at Rangoon from the north.

He also knew that the huge logistical nightmare associated with relying on land-based lines of communication could in large part be overcome by the use of air supply, a factor that had played a significant part in smashing both *U-Go* and *Ha-Go* during the previous six months. Although still a relatively scarce resource, he now had access to many more aircraft than a year before. If he could plan on their use to sustain offensive operations across the Chindwin, the over-long lines of communication (previously a limiting factor in the consideration of offensive land-based operations into Burma) could be ameliorated.

He found himself faced with his second great chance and he was determined to seize it. The first task was to get to the Chindwin and seize crossings over the river. The British 2nd Division took Tamu on 4 August. The large village provided Slim with access to the Chindwin via the road (laid

Engineers jerry-rig a bridge in Burma. (Victoria State Archives)

out by British troops in 1887) to Sittaung and Kalemyo, as well as the Kabaw Valley. With its precious airfield, Tamu offered the Allies the air dominance that was essential to Fourteenth Army's advance.

Slim now reorganized his army, ready for the push to the Chindwin. The 17th and 23rd Indian divisions (together with HQ IV Corps) were sent back to India for rest. 3 Commando Brigade, which had been responsible during the siege of Imphal for guarding the Silchar Track, returned to Arakan to support planned operations against Akyab by XV Corps; and 2nd, 7th and 20th Indian divisions were sent to be rested in the Imphal Plain. The 11th East African Division (21st, 25th and 26th brigades), which had just moved into Imphal, came forward to relieve 23rd Indian Division.

On 6 August 1944 Slim ordered Stopford, who with his XXXIII Corps now had responsibility for all operations east of the Manipur River, to direct his pursuit to Kalewa and Sittaung on the Chindwin via both Tamu and Tiddim. The 5th Indian Division advanced down the Tiddim Road, while 11th East African Division led the advance from Tamu towards both Sittaung and Kalemyo on the river, where both divisions were to converge. They methodically pushed their way against last-ditch opposition to the Chindwin. The process was slow and difficult because of continuing Japanese resistance, the appalling monsoon weather and difficult terrain. Men, mules and elephants struggled down jungle tracks after the retreating Japanese, crossing swollen rivers and rebuilding collapsed tracks and roads. The division was sustained exclusively by air. The over-stretched air forces pushed through minimal visibility to deliver their precious loads by parachute and free drop to the troops below them.

The East Africans occupied Sittaung on 4 September, and by 10 September the Chindwin was crossed and a small bridgehead secured. Four weeks later a second crossing was established, again by the East Africans, at Mawlaik. The 5th Indian Division's task on the Tiddim front against the still-dangerous remnants of 33rd Division was made immeasurably easier by the activities of the semi-irregular Lushai Brigade. This British-officered force of Indian soldiers and Chin levies proved to be very successful in harassing the flanks of the retreating Japanese. Slim regarded the brigade's exploits to be the epitome of successful long-range guerrilla operations, with a significant strategic effect in terms of its contribution to deciding the shape of the battle-scape that Slim was trying to design. 'As an example of effective Long-Range Penetration through "impossible" country its operation had never been surpassed,' he wrote in a summary of the campaign published in Australia in 1950.

After a hard slog down the road, 5th Indian Division occupied Tiddim on 17 October.

The Japanese fought hard to stop the advance at the 8,800ft Kennedy Peak, but they were unsuccessful in bloody fighting in atrocious weather. On 13 November, 5th Indian and 11th East African divisions joined hands at Kalemyo, the Africans having progressively removed Japanese opposition in the Kabaw Valley. The fighting had been torturous. The monsoon remained in full spate. Japanese rear-guards fought to the death, holding up the advance with snipers, mines and ambushes, requiring a slow, methodical clearance. Malaria remained a killer. Despite these impediments, the East African division seized Kalewa on 2 December. The main crossing point for Fourteenth Army was now in Allied hands. By 10 December, in an extraordinary logistical and engineering achievement, sappers erected the largest Bailey bridge then in existence – 1,154ft long – across the river. The Chindwin, the first great obstacle to Fourteenth Army entering Burma, had been bridged.

Soldiers of IV Corps rest with their mules after crossing the Chindwin River near Sittaung before pushing east to link up with 36th Division, 17 November 1944. With the roads unsuitable for heavy traffic, and the railway bridges damaged, resupply and further movement was a major challenge. Mules were a vital tool in moving supplies through the jungle. (Imperial War Museums via Getty Images)

At the same time, the long NCAC advance from Ledo towards Myitkyina, which had begun at the end of 1943, captured Myitkyina with the help of the rump of the Chindits from Operation *Thursday*. Holding Myitkyina, with its airfield and railhead, was a crucial element in the strategy to create a new Burma Road. The battle for Myitkyina began well, with the capture of the airfield by the American Galahad Force on 16 May 1944. The Japanese (18th Division) fought ferociously until early August, after which the town was fully in Allied hands. A start could then be made by the British 36th Division under Major-General Francis Festing to begin the march south towards Indaw and Mandalay, along what was known as the Railway Corridor. All being well, an offensive into Upper Burma from Manipur would join up with 36th Division along the banks of the Irrawaddy north of Mandalay.

For the offensive into Burma, Slim's army (XV Corps in Arakan now temporarily reporting directly to General Sir Oliver Leese, Giffard's replacement) comprised six infantry divisions, two tank brigades and three independent infantry brigades – a combat force of close to 90,000 men. However, logistical realities meant that Slim would only be able to deploy two offensive corps for Operation *Capital*, comprising four infantry divisions (three Indian and one British), two tank brigades and two independent infantry brigades – a force of close to 60,000 men, or only 65 per cent of what he had available. The army reserve of two divisions (one Indian and one East African) and two infantry brigades (one of which, the Lushai Brigade, was not intended for operations outside of its own territory) would remain on the Chindwin. The composition of the two corps is given below:

IV Corps (Lieutenant-General Frank Messervy, from 8 December 1944)
    7th Indian Division (Major-General Geoffrey Evans)
    17th Indian Division (Major-General David 'Punch' Cowan)
    19th Indian Division (Major-General Pete 'Chota' Rees)
    255th Tank Brigade (Brigadier Claude Pert), equipped with Sherman tanks
XXXIII Corps (Lieutenant-General Sir Montagu Stopford)
    British 2nd Division (Major-General Graham Nicholson)
    20th Indian Division (Major-General Douglas Gracey)
    268th Indian Infantry Brigade (Brigadier Godfrey Dyer)
    254th Tank Brigade (Brigadier Reginald Scoones), equipped with M3 Stuart and Lee-Grant tanks
Army Reserve (remaining on the Chindwin)
    5th Indian Division (Major-General Dermot Warren)
    1st East African Division (Major-General Charles Fowkes, until January 1945; Major-General Bob Mansergh, January–February 1945; Major-General William Dimoline, February–May 1945)
    28th East African Brigade (Brigadier Bob Mansergh, until February 1945)
    Lushai Brigade (Brigadier Philip C. Marindin)

The vast distances involved in moving even 65 per cent of his army beyond the Chindwin to the Shwebo Plain meant that Operation *Capital* was always going to be a war of logistics for Slim as much as it would be a battlefield confrontation with General Heitaro Kimura's army. He was faced with fighting a numerically superior enemy at the end of a line of communication that would only grow in length and complexity with every mile he advanced. The vast distances involved were the principal brake on

Aerial resupply was fundamental to Allied operations in 1944 and 1945. In 1945, 90 per cent of the combat supplies for IV Corps were delivered by air. (Victoria State Archives)

Allied operations. All troops and equipment had either to come over the Naga Hills from Dimapur and thence to Tamu and Kalewa, or by air into Imphal, or, once it had been captured, Tamu. As airfields were captured during the offensive, they could be pressed into service. The problem with aerial resupply was that an attack on the Japanese on the other side of the Irrawaddy (Mandalay or Meiktila) would outstrip the economical flying range (250 miles) of transport aircraft based at Imphal. Slim would have to win the land battle along the Irrawaddy in order to capture the airfields necessary for the resupply and continued progress of Fourteenth Army towards Rangoon, although a small fleet of homemade boats on the Chindwin would help immensely with ferrying stores, vehicles and troops.

To match the new style of fighting that Slim expected once the Chindwin and Irrawaddy had been crossed, Slim appointed Frank Messervy and Montagu Stopford as his two corps commanders. The two men would, he knew, thrive under his type of leadership. Stopford had driven XXXIII Corps through the Kohima battles to the Chindwin. In planning the offensive, Slim was concerned to tell Messervy and Stopford what to do, while allowing them virtually complete freedom to decide how they carried out his instructions.

In Burma this approach to command made especial sense, for two reasons. First, the geographical difficulties in the theatre made regular communication difficult. More importantly, he believed that his commanders could best achieve his requirements without him breathing down their necks while they were conducting operations. 'My corps and divisions were called upon to act with at least as much freedom as armies and corps in other theatres,' he recalled. 'Commanders at all levels had to act more on their own; they were given greater latitude to work out their own plans to achieve what they knew was the Army Commander's intention. In time they developed to a marked degree a flexibility of mind and a firmness of decision that enabled them to act swiftly to take advantage of sudden information or changing circumstances without reference to their superiors.'

Slim's plan for Operation *Capital* necessitated the retraining and restructuring of his army. Once over the Irrawaddy, the army would have to fight in a very different style to that which had won it victories in Arakan, and at Imphal and Kohima. After two long years of jungle fighting, the wide prairie-like plains of Central Burma beckoned, where fast-moving armoured thrusts, large-scale artillery 'stonks' and attacks on broad fronts by brigades and divisions would replace the intense but relatively slow bayonet, rifle and grenade struggles by sections, platoons and companies in the half-gloom of the wet jungle that had characterized the fighting in Arakan and the hills of eastern India. Speed, the massed use of armour, bold flanking movements and the close cooperation of tanks, infantry, artillery and aircraft would define operations in this new environment. Messervy suggested, among other things, that one brigade of 17th Indian Division be mechanized and another made air-transportable to exploit the new terrain. Slim agreed and converted 5th Indian Division to the new organization as well. Messervy's idea proved critical both to the seizure of Meiktila the following February and in the epic dash to Rangoon that followed. Likewise, the armoured brigades were re-equipped with medium tanks (Shermans in one and Lee-Grants in the other) and an infantry battalion, carried in armoured vehicles, added to each. To each armoured squadron was added a troop of flame-throwers. There weren't enough British self-propelled artillery pieces available for Burma, so General Sir Claude Auchinleck (Commander-in-Chief India) had gratefully accepted the offer of surplus American 105mm 'Priests'. Despite the different calibre of the ammunition this entailed, the logistical nuisance of having another calibre of artillery ammunition to haul to the front was offset by the tactical flexibility motorized artillery was able to offer Messervy in the forthcoming battles. In September and October 1944, considerable retraining took place in Fourteenth Army to prepare for this new style of warfighting.

During the pursuit to the Chindwin, Slim had been exercised about how he could engage and defeat General Katamura's Fifteenth Army in open battle once the Chindwin had been breached. Intelligence had shown that the Japanese had built up substantial stocks of war materiel on the Shwebo Plain, giving a strong indication that General Kimura wished to fight his defensive battle for Mandalay to the north of the great river. This was correct. Katamura's orders in October 1944 were to ensure any enemy advance did not manage to cross the Irrawaddy, Fifteenth Army securing in Operation *Ban* the area north of Madaya, Sagaing and Pakokku. This suited Slim. The vast Shwebo Plain was the ideal terrain for the battle he sought – a battle of manoeuvre in which his artillery, armour (including the newly arrived Sherman tanks of 254th and 255th Armoured brigades) and air support would have a devastating effect on the Japanese, 'where tanks would operate in quantities instead of by twos or threes, where guns must be

Two British 'Lifebuoy' flame-thrower operators move forward to rout out Japanese foxholes. Flame-throwers were deployed by men of the British 36th Division in the Railway Corridor (between Mogaung and Indaw) north of Mandalay in late 1944. (Mirrorpix via Getty Images)

The Lee-Grant tank 'Caledonian' in Mandalay, March 1945. (Victoria State Archives)

capable of fire and movement, where infantry must manoeuvre fast and far'. Slim believed that Kimura would want to prevent the Allies from dominating the vast space on the western side of the Irrawaddy, even though it would mean that the Japanese would be forced to fight with their backs to the river, in country suited to the type of warfare that did not favour them: a fast-moving series of armour-dominated engagements where the Allied armour, aircraft and artillery would relatively easily discomfit the infantry-dominated Japanese forces. Slim assumed that the typical Japanese fear of withdrawal would mean that Kimura – a commander he did not know, but whom he assumed would be similar to all other Japanese generals of his acquaintance – would not withdraw behind the Irrawaddy as it would be tantamount to admitting failure.

The Shwebo Plain was 400 miles from the nearest railhead at Dimapur, with a single-track earthen road for 250 miles of it that was impassable in the monsoon. Slim's two corps were outnumbered by Kimura's forces which, though chastened, were far from beaten. But Fourteenth Army's advantage in the air, in armour, its greater mobility in the open, and the spirit of its troops gave him the confidence to press ahead despite what otherwise would have appeared to be unacceptable odds. Slim's assessment was that the battered remnants of Fifteenth Army would hold a defensive line in the formidable jungle-clad mountains of the Zibyu Taungdam Range. It's what he would have done; holding his troops back on the high ground, waiting to see where the enemy crossed the Chindwin and responding with counter-thrusts accordingly. This range of hills lay about 25 miles to the east of the Chindwin and ran parallel to it for a distance of 120 miles. Slim's plan was to punch through them with Messervy's IV Corps on the left and General Stopford's XXXIII Corps on the right, both corps converging on the area of Ye-U–Shwebo. The plan was for IV Corps to break out of the Sittaung bridgehead and, following an easterly course, force its way through the mountains, seize Pinlebu and thereafter change direction to capture Shwebo from the north. Stopford's XXXIII Corps, meanwhile, would advance from Kalewa on a broad front, following the general south-easterly route of the Chindwin towards Ye-U and Monywa.

THE CAMPAIGN

OPERATION *CAPITAL*

Wasting no time, Fourteenth Army crossed the Chindwin as soon as it was reached. Slim urged Messervy to advance as quickly as possible and to take risks that would months before have been unthinkable, in order to maintain the momentum of the advance. The IV Corps advance was led by Major-General Peter Rees's 19th Indian Division. Moving out of Sittaung on 4 December, the division headed for Pinlebu, 60 miles to the east. Rees, driving his units on, made rapid progress through the Zibyu Taungdam Hills. A diminutive and popular Welshman, Rees epitomized the type of divisional commander that Slim had spent so long cultivating in Fourteenth Army. Less than two weeks after the advance had begun, Rees had joined his division up with Major-General Francis Festing's 36th Division at Rail Indaw, 90 miles east of Sittaung, part of the NCAC's successful drive south from Lashio against Thirty-Third Army.

Throughout, Japanese resistance was far less intense than had been expected. Nevertheless, Rees's advance was an extraordinary effort given the appalling nature of the terrain. Roads had to be hacked out of the virgin jungle by troops using what tools they could carry. Farther south, a brigade of 20th Indian Division led the XXXIII Corps advance, crossing the Chindwin north of Kalewa at Mawlaik, while 11th East African Division fought hard to extend the bridgehead at Kalewa. On 18 December, the remainder of 20th Indian Division followed through the bridgehead. During December, leading formations of Fourteenth Army advanced eastwards from their bridgeheads across the Chindwin. In the face of fierce opposition, 2nd Division captured Kaduma and on 31 December seized the Kabo Weir on the Mu River, preventing the Japanese from destroying this key part of the Shwebo Plain irrigation system. The XXXIII Corps now had a firm footing in the centre of the Shwebo Plain.

Men of the Royal Welsh Fusiliers, part of the British 36th Division which fought down the Railway Corridor from Mogaung to Indaw and Mandalay, patrol near Pinbaw, north of Hopin, December 1944. (Imperial War Museum)

Indian troops hitch a ride on a Stuart tank in the advance by XXXIII Corps to the Chindwin, November 1944. (AFP via Getty Images)

Within days of the start of IV Corps' advance, however, Slim accepted that his initial plan to trap Katamura's Fifteenth Army on the Shwebo Plain in front of the Irrawaddy would not work. The weakness of the opposition facing 19th Indian Division forced him to recognize that Katamura had withdrawn the bulk of his forces east of the Irrawaddy, with the obvious intention of fighting behind, rather than in front of, the river. If this were to happen, Fourteenth Army would be stretched out from Tamu and vulnerable to counter-attack just when it was attempting to cross one of the most formidable river barriers imaginable. Slim's original expectation that General Kimura would be content to meet Fourteenth Army on terms distinctly disadvantageous to himself was, perhaps, unduly optimistic. In any case, Kimura's withdrawal behind the Irrawaddy dashed this expectation. But fighting Kimura on the eastern and southern side of the Irrawaddy, after having first crossed the river, was never considered a sensible option. It would mean dealing with Burma Area Army's concentrated forces just at the point where Fourteenth Army was most vulnerable and the Japanese at their strongest. Slim believed that while the strategy for winning back Burma was frontal, and resolutely engaging the might of the Burma Area Army, the operational design for doing so must not be.

British soldiers of 36th Division being treated by US Army medics at Pinwe, 12 November 1944. (Corbis via Getty Images)

Instead, Slim sought a means of not just crossing his five divisions and three tank brigades without mishap or significant interference over the Irrawaddy but of creating the decisive advantage he required to bring the Japanese to battle on his own terms. He wanted to attack Kimura where the enemy forces were weakest, and where he could deploy his armoured and air-supported forces to greatest effect. Crossing the Irrawaddy in the teeth of the Japanese defence of the river would lack subtlety, fail to use the opportunity for surprise and would risk large numbers of unnecessary casualties. Could he attack the enemy somewhere other than his most heavily defended part? Slim's eyes turned to the towns of Meiktila and Thazi, lying approximately 70 miles south of Mandalay. These towns were the key nodal points on Kimura's line of communication supporting both Thirty-Third and Fifteenth armies. They were the beating heart of the Burma Area Army. The towns represented ground that was vital to the enemy defence, a concept Fourteenth Army had first learned painfully in Arakan. The railway and main road from Rangoon ran through Meiktila before bending north on their way to Mandalay, and the town formed a natural location for supply and ammunition dumps, airfields and hospitals. If Slim could cut off both Honda and Katamura's corps from this vital logistical centre, the Japanese ability to resist XXXIII Corps' inexorable pressure in the north around Mandalay would be fatally weakened. Slim recognized that without Meiktila, Kimura could not hope to sustain a prolonged battle for Mandalay. Indeed, it might even prove to be the decisive act in the destruction of the whole of Kimura's army.

Within days, Slim and his staff had come up with a plan, which was dubbed Operation *Extended Capital*. The idea was to make Kimura believe that nothing had changed, that Fourteenth Army's advance remained focused on Mandalay with XXXIII Corps and IV Corps crossing the Irrawaddy north-west of the city. The essence of Slim's new plan, however, was that while XXXIII Corps would continue to cross the Irrawaddy to the north of Mandalay as originally planned, the reconfigured IV Corps (Geoffrey Evans' 7th and 'Punch' Cowan's 17th Indian divisions, newly returned from rest, together with 28th East African Brigade, 255th Tank Brigade and the Lushai Brigade) would instead cross the Irrawaddy in great secrecy far to the south in the area of Pakokku. It would then strike hard with armour, motorized artillery and infantry at Meiktila. The northern advance by XXXIII Corps (strengthened by 19th Indian Division and 268th Tank Brigade) would be a

Troops of the 11th East African Division crossing the Chindwin at Shwegyin, December 1944. (Imperial War Museums via Getty Images)

deception to hide the decisive strike by IV Corps to the south. If Slim could attract the greatest possible number of enemy divisions towards the northern crossing points (where, after all, Kimura expected him to strike), he could minimize opposition to the real focus of his attack in the south. This would provide Slim with, as he put it, 'not only the major battle I desired, but the chance to repeat our old hammer and anvil tactics: XXXIII Corps the hammer from the north against the anvil of IV Corps at Meiktila – and the Japanese between.' Had the aircraft been available, Slim would have employed parachute forces to capture Meiktila, to hold the airfield for his air-transportable divisions to land in the heart of the enemy.

Loading supplies onto a
Douglas C-47 Dakota transport.
(Victoria State Archives)

Slim explained his revised plan to Messervy and Stopford on 18 December, and on 19 December issued his plan. On 17 December he had sent a summary of his intentions to Leese, and on 20 December he sent a full copy of the plan to HQ ALFSEA. On 26 December Slim moved his formations in accordance with his new plan, 268th Brigade and 19th Indian Division transferring from IV Corps to XXXIII Corps. The speed at which Slim made these changes left little time for wide consultation. He regarded his change of plan to be within the wider remit he had been given, and thus decided to inform Leese of what he intended rather than seeking his permission. Messervy and Stopford quickly translated Slim's revised plan into action and XXXIII Corps' advance continued unabated during this period.

Chinese troops in US-supplied
Sherman tanks move forward
in January 1945. (Hulton-
Deutsch Collection/Corbis via
Getty Images)

The leading troops of 2nd Division, together with the Lee-Grant and Stuart tanks of 254th Tank Brigade, passed through Pyingaing (known to the troops as 'Pink Gin') on 23 December. Japanese rearguards attempted to hold up the advance through ambushes and mines. Ye-U and its airfield were captured on 2 January 1945 and by 5 January the division had established a firm bridgehead over the Mu River. The British 2nd Division and 19th Indian Division now began a race for Shwebo, with Katamura's 15th Division streaming before it in full retreat to the Irrawaddy. Shwebo was captured on 9 January jointly by units of both divisions. Rees' 19th Indian Division reached the Shwebo area by 5 January, established bridgeheads over the Irrawaddy at Thabeikkyin and Kyaukyaung and began to advance southward on the east bank of the river towards Mandalay.

An Indian mule train crosses a Burmese river using a Bailey Bridge. (Victoria State Archives)

Slim's plan was bold. Surprise and secrecy were essential. But the advance depended entirely on Slim's ability to supply his armoured spearheads as they penetrated deep into Japanese-held territory. The administrative effort to supply two corps well forward of their supply bases in inhospitable terrain was formidable. XXXIII Corps had to push rapidly forward in the north, while IV Corps, with its armour, moved in secret down 330 miles of rough dirt track from Tamu to the area of Pakokku before conducting an opposed crossing of one of the world's mightiest rivers. 'We were, in fact, defying some of the principles of war in undertaking the reconquest of Burma from the north to the south – as the strategic situation compelled us to do – instead of in the reverse direction,' wrote Leese in May 1945. 'Thus our main line of communication ran at right-angles to the enemy, while we were operating in reverse to, and against the trend of the main river and road arteries of the country. The distances were very great, existing communications were poor, and both climate and terrain were unfavourable.'

The physical restraint of operating in difficult terrain at long distances from railheads meant that Slim was able to sustain over the Chindwin no more than four and two-thirds divisions and two tank brigades. However, the decisive advantage the Allies enjoyed in the air meant that he could rely on air transport to maintain his forward units, so long as the requisite numbers of aircraft remained available. With the vast experience of the Battle of the Admin Box in Arakan in February 1944, of Operation *Thursday* and of Operation *Stamina* (the airlift to Imphal during the siege in 1944), the air supply organization supporting Fourteenth Army had become highly efficient. But having sufficient aircraft available remained a constant headache. Slim's plans were dealt a devastating blow on the morning of 10 December 1944 when he awoke at Imphal to the sound of mass aircraft activity at the nearby airfield. He quickly discovered that 75 of his precious USAAF C-47s were being diverted to meet a developing crisis in China. The Japanese *Ichi-Go* offensive directed against 14th USAAF's air bases in China (about which Stilwell had repeatedly warned) was proceeding well and threatened to reach

Men of the 11th East African Division on the road to Kalewa, on the Chindwin, January 1945. (AFP via Getty Images)

Kunming. If this happened, the entire Hump operation would be unseated. The chiefs of staff ordered two of the Chinese divisions to return to China, together with three Combat Cargo squadrons, each of 25 aircraft. Slim immediately told Mountbatten that without these aircraft the success of Operation *Capital* could not be guaranteed. Mountbatten fought hard to have the aircraft returned, and on 21 January two of the three squadrons Slim had lost (i.e. 50 aircraft) were returned to him. By this time anyway, Slim's troops were well across the Irrawaddy and the prospect of the road from Ledo opening up, and consigning the Hump to history, was quickly beckoning. Nevertheless, it was estimated that Slim needed 140 transport aircraft permanently allocated to Fourteenth Army to keep his troops on the move. By cajoling the Joint Chiefs of Staff in London, Mountbatten managed to secure a further 30 aircraft destined to support the newly created British Pacific Fleet, and 25 C-47s diverted from the Mediterranean Theatre. Slim ended up with 145 aircraft, albeit three weeks later than he had hoped, but in time to deal what he hoped would be a decisive blow against Meiktila and Mandalay.

But while air transport answered some of Slim's most pressing needs, the enormous land-based line of communication also required substantial work to ensure that Fourteenth Army could operate far ahead of its bases in Assam. It was 506 miles from the Fourteenth Army depot at Dimapur to Mandalay, the line of communication running through Imphal, Tamu, Kalewa, Shwebo and Mandalay. Road-building and upgrading was essential, but limited resources restricted what could be done. This constant crisis of resources, however, had a positive effect on the men of Fourteenth Army. It forced them to become self-reliant and innovative. 'With us' Slim recalled, 'necessity was the mother of invention. We lacked so much in equipment and supplies that, if we were not to give up offensive operations altogether, we had either to manage without or improvise for ourselves … my soldiers forced the opposed crossing of great rivers using inadequate equipment, stretched brittle communication links to fantastic lengths, marched over the most heart-breaking country on reduced rations, fought disease with discipline to beat it.' Slim's chief engineer, Bill Hasted, felled forests alongside the Chindwin at Kalewa to make barges able to take 10 tons each, in order to make best use of the Chindwin as a supply artery. Three of these tied together could carry a Sherman tank. An extraordinary 541 were built. Outboard engines were flown in, boat wrecks were repaired and even sunken vessels on the riverbed were recovered, repaired and pressed

Gurkhas hold onto their mules as they swim across the Irrawaddy River en route to Mandalay, 27 January 1945. (Imperial War Museums via Getty Images)

into service. These and other measures were so successful that whereas in November 1943 an average of 2,800 tons a day was moved forward, by September 1944 this had increased to 6,500 tons and by March 1945 nearly 9,000 tons a day. To protect this now vital river line of communication two homemade (but leaky) 12-knot armed patrol vessels were built on the banks of the Chindwin at Kalewa, which Slim unofficially commissioned HMS *Una* (after his daughter) and HMS *Pamela* (after Mountbatten's daughter). By March 1945 these vessels were protecting an inland water transport system carrying up to 700 tons of men and materiel a day on both the Chindwin and Irrawaddy rivers. It was a remarkable logistical achievement.

Gurkha soldiers exit the Irrawaddy on 27 January. (Universal Images Group via Getty Images)

Messervy's IV Corps began its secret march south down the Myittha Valley (also known as the Gangaw Valley) on 19 January, and despite the difficulties of the terrain moved quickly. Slim had given Messervy 15 February as the last acceptable date for crossing the Irrawaddy. Elaborate deception measures were adopted to ensure that Messervy's move through the jungle to Pakokku remained concealed from the Japanese, and to reinforce in Kimura's mind the certain belief that IV Corps remained with XXXIII Corps on the Shwebo Plain, preparing to cross the

Infantry from the Chinese 22nd Division advance through the jungle during the southward push from the Irrawaddy River. (Imperial War Museums via Getty Images)

river above Mandalay. While the real IV Corps had to keep radio silence during its move southwards, a dummy corps headquarters was established in Tamu, using the same radio frequencies, through which all communications from 19th Indian Division to XXXIII Corps had to pass. Despite the inconvenience this caused for commanders this complicated deception was spectacularly successful. The signals intelligence capability that had served Slim so well at Imphal and Kohima accompanied Fourteenth Army on the advance into Burma, a 300-strong Special Wireless Group being attached to Slim's headquarters, and travelling with it, from Comilla, to Monywa and then Meiktila. Each of IV Corps and XXXIII Corps (and XV Corps in Arakan) had an attached Special Wireless Company, all for the purpose of immediately decoding enemy battlefield communications.

The Japanese did not believe that a large-scale advance through the Gangaw Valley was possible and never seriously considered it. In order to help reinforce these perceptions, Messervy, when his advance reached the town of Gangaw, arranged with Slim for the town's defences to be overwhelmingly attacked on 10 January by the Strategic Air Force with follow-up occupation by the Lushai Brigade, rather than using his divisions for the purpose. Using the latter would have demonstrated to the Japanese that Slim's division were on the march far from where they were expected. Unobserved and unhindered Messervy's forward units reached Pauk, 40 miles from Pakokku, in late January. Kimura, while aware of some activity on his southern flank, regarded this to be nothing more than demonstrations by minor forces designed to draw him south, and he was not to be tempted into doing something so foolish. All the while he continued to reinforce the Irrawaddy in the Mandalay area, bringing in all available forces from across Burma, so that by February he had a force equivalent to eight Japanese and

Fourteenth Army's advance to the Irrawaddy, December 1944–March 1945

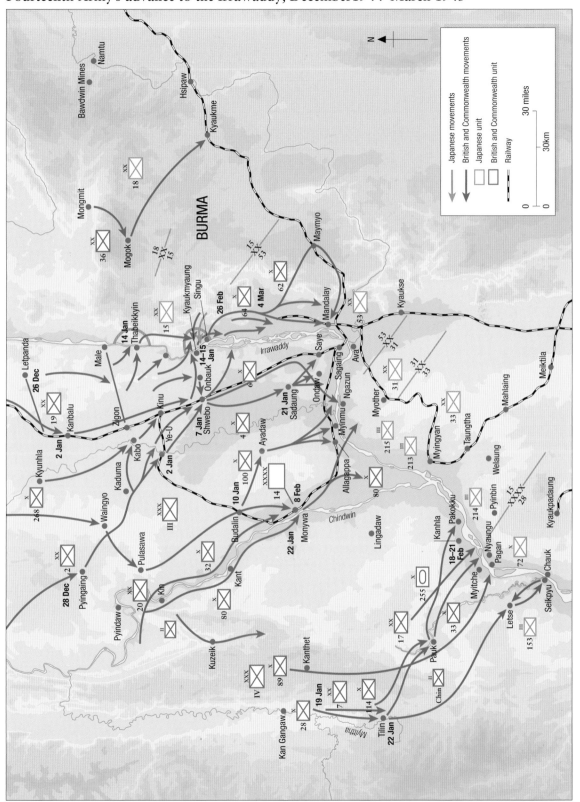

one-and-a-third INA divisions. He was confident that these would be more than sufficient to defeat the expected five divisions of Fourteenth Army in what he was now calling the decisive 'Battle of the Irrawaddy Shore'. His failure to appreciate the overall subtlety of Slim's approach, the dynamism and mobility of his army, together with the extraordinary power and flexibility afforded to Slim by virtue of air superiority and air transport, proved to be the major strands in his undoing.

In Burma, one man above all others could see the writing on the wall for the Japanese. The Allies received news on 1 January 1945 that the Burmese military leader General Aung San and his Burma National Army (BNA) would be prepared to switch sides. An operation by Special Operations Executive (SOE) – codenamed *Nation* – was launched to liaise with the BNA and the leadership of another group, the Anti-Fascist Organization (AFO), and so facilitate this delicate transfer of loyalties. The first parachute drop of agents was to Toungoo on 27 January and comprised an all-Burma force. It reported that the BNA – or significant parts of it – was ready to turn, but that the AFO needed arming. A team parachuted into Burma on 20 March reported that action by the BNA would begin in a week.

THE MASTERSTROKE AT MEIKTILA

In Central Burma the advantage was now Slim's: only six weeks after he had changed his plan Fourteenth Army was on the shores of the Irrawaddy on a 200-mile front with IV Corps about to cross the river in the south, in the area of Pakokku. The advance of Fourteenth Army had been so rapid that Mountbatten reported to London on 23 February 1945 that Operation *Dracula* would no longer be required: Slim appeared likely to seize Rangoon before the onset of the monsoon in May. With XXXIII Corps placing growing pressure on the Japanese in the area of Mandalay, the timing of the main crossings became increasingly crucial. Too soon and Kimura would recognize the threat to his southern flank and deploy his reserves to counter it: too late and the pressure on XXXIII Corps might be sufficient to halt its advance on Mandalay altogether.

Indian armour of 255th Tank Brigade prepares to assault Meiktila, February 1945. (Imperial War Museum)

In early February Stopford made successive and determined efforts from the north to capture Mandalay, reinforcing the impression that this was Slim's point of main effort. Katamura threw the 15th, 53rd and elements of both 31st and 33rd divisions into the attack at the 19th Indian Division bridgehead at Thabeikkyin. Kimura, agreeing with Katamura's assessment that this was the likely location of Fourteenth Army's principal attack, gave Katamura additional artillery and some of his remaining tanks. However, it was to no avail: as the bridgehead strengthened, the Japanese were slowly pushed back despite heavy Japanese artillery attacks. No. 221 Group RAF provided continuous and effective close air support to 19th Indian Division as it built itself up on the eastern bank of the Irrawaddy.

British infantry search village huts on the outskirts of Meiktila, March 1945. (Imperial War Museum)

Meanwhile Gracey's 20th Indian Division approached Monywa and took the town after hard fighting in mid-January. On 8 February Slim moved his and Air Vice Marshal Vincent's joint headquarters to the town that he had vacated during the retreat from Burma in May 1942. Other troops from 20th Indian Division arrived at Allagappa and began to cross the Irrawaddy on the night of 12 February. The Japanese were slow to oppose this incursion, but when they did, it was with desperate fury, waves of attacks taking place during the ensuing fortnight against the two bridgeheads, many during daylight. Gracey had chosen to cross at a point that marked the divisional boundary between the Japanese 31st and 33rd divisions, which caused some confusion in Japanese command, but Kimura reacted strongly when he realized that a second – unexpected – bridgehead was in progress. Again, Allied air power played a decisive role in defeating these counter-attacks, the Hurribombers of No. 221 Group destroying the tanks of Kimura's sole armoured regiment in Burma. In losing air superiority, Kimura's remaining mechanized forces became easy targets for Allied aircraft soaring at will over the Mandalay skies.

Despite the second bridgehead at Allagappa, Kimura believed that the Allied advance into Upper Burma was progressing as he envisaged. An advance into the Shwebo Plain preparatory to an assault across the Irrawaddy, west and north of Mandalay, was the natural course for an enemy attack on Mandalay. He knew that the American-led NCAC forces were advancing in the north from Myitkyina; a convergence of these with Fourteenth Army prior to an attack on Mandalay from the north was what he was expecting. His decision not to risk engaging Fourteenth Army on the Shwebo Plain coincided with orders from Tokyo to consider the land route to China to be of secondary importance to the need to protect Southern Burma and Rangoon. It was a simple step to deduce that Mandalay needed reinforcement, to prevent the Allies from capturing the city and using it to move into Central Burma. Accordingly, he restructured the Burma Area Army to enable him to fight the decisive battle for Burma on the Irrawaddy

shore – i.e. at Mandalay. First, he withdrew 18th Division, a regiment from 2nd Division and a regiment from 49th Division – in all the equivalent of close-on two divisions – from his Northern Front to reinforce the Central Front, the defence of which centred on Mandalay. He next withdrew the remnants of 54th Division from Arakan and positioned it on the Irrawaddy at Yenangyaung. This would serve to resist any opportunist movement by the Allies on the Allied right flank. Finally, 49th Division was moved up from the Bassein Peninsula in the far south-west of the country, and a further regiment of 2nd Division, en route to Indochina, was ordered to return. From Yenangyaung in the south to Mandalay in the north, Kimura was confident that his nine divisions (which included an INA division) sitting behind the Irrawaddy would be sufficient to smash any attempt by Fourteenth Army to cross and win a decisive victory for Mandalay. In numbers alone, he was right to be confident.

The real focus of Slim's offensive, of course, entirely unbeknown to Kimura, lay far to the south. With Kimura distracted by XXXIII Corps' operations in the north, final preparations were being made, in conditions of strict secrecy, for the rapier thrust to seize Meiktila. If Kimura gained any inkling of this threat to his rear area, all would be undone. The first crossings by Geoffrey Evans' 7th Indian Division began at Nyaungu on the night of 13 February. It took four days to establish a bridgehead, 6,000 yards wide by 4,000 yards deep. Feverish activity then followed to feed the assault formations across the river by boat and barge – Sherman tanks in their scores floating across on homemade pontoons – and to prepare them for the breakout. Messervy's plan for the dash to Meiktila had six phases:

1.   The exploitation east from the Nyaungu bridgehead by the two mechanized brigades of 17th Indian Division and 255th Indian Tank Brigade.

2.   The concentration of these forces at Mahlaing.

3.   The capture of the airstrip at Thabutkon to fly in 99th Brigade.

4.   The isolation of Meiktila.

5.   The capture of Meiktila.

6.   The capture of Thazi.

Messervy's plan was that two brigades (63rd and 48th) of 17th Indian Division, together with the Sherman tanks of 255th Tank Brigade, would

Northern Combat Area Command operations, 1944–45

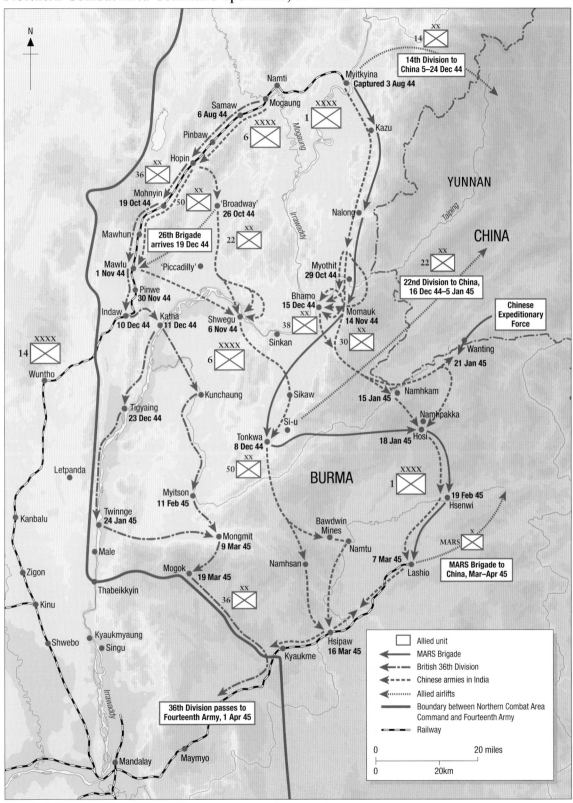

N

14th Division to China 5–24 Dec 44

Myitkyina **Captured 3 Aug 44**

Namti

Samaw **6 Aug 44**

Mogaung

Pinbaw

Kazu

Hopin

36 Mohnyin **19 Oct 44**

50 'Broadway' **26 Oct 44**

26th Brigade arrives 19 Dec 44

22

YUNNAN

CHINA

Mawhun

Mawlu **1 Nov 44**

'Piccadilly'

Myothit **29 Oct 44**

22 **22nd Division to China, 16 Dec 44–5 Jan 45**

Pinwe **30 Nov 44**

Bhamo **15 Dec 44**

Momauk **14 Nov 44**

Chinese Expeditionary Force

Indaw **10 Dec 44**

Katha **11 Dec 44**

Shwegu **6 Nov 44**

38

30

Wanting **21 Jan 45**

6

Sinkan

14

Wuntho

6

Kunchaung

Sikaw

Si-u

15 Jan 45

Namhkam

Namhpakka

Tigyaing **23 Dec 44**

Tonkwa **8 Dec 44**

18 Jan 45

Hosi

Letpanda

50

BURMA

1

19 Feb 45

Hsenwi

Myitson **11 Feb 45**

Bawdwin Mines

MARS

Kanbalu

Twinnge **24 Jan 45**

Mongmit **9 Mar 45**

Namtu

7 Mar 45

MARS Brigade to China, Mar–Apr 45

Male

Namhsan

Lashio

Zigon

Mogok **19 Mar 45**

Kinu

Thabeikkyin

36

Shwebo

Kyaukmyaung

Singu

Hsipaw **16 Mar 45**

Kyaukme

36th Division passes to Fourteenth Army, 1 Apr 45

Irrawaddy

Mandalay

Maymyo

	Allied unit
◀━	MARS Brigade
◀·━·◀	British 36th Division
◀----	Chinese armies in India
◀·······	Allied airlifts
━━	Boundary between Northern Combat Area Command and Fourteenth Army
━┼━┼━	Railway

0   20 miles

0   20km

49

Infantry from 6th Gurkha Rifles (Slim's old regiment) advance behind armour at Singu, February 1945. (Victoria State Archives)

cross the river to seize Meiktila. He needed to capture the town as quickly as possible without worrying about securing the road behind him. The road would subsequently be cleared by 7th Indian Division once the security of the Irrawaddy bridgehead was firm. Cowan's plan was to use his armour to punch through the Japanese lines to seize an airfield at Thabutkon, 12 miles east of Meiktila. He would then fly in 17th Indian Division's third (air-transportable) brigade – 99th Brigade – while Taungtha and Mahlaing were either captured or screened by his other two brigades. The whole division with the armour would then continue on to assault Meiktila.

Elaborate deception measures were adopted to cover the Nyaungu crossings. The 28th East African Brigade pretended to parry south to recover the Chauk and Yenangyaung oilfields, dummy parachute drops were made east of Chauk to reinforce this picture and 17th Indian Division applied heavy pressure on Pakokku to make out that crossings were also intended there. These deception schemes were undoubtedly successful and acted to hide, until it was too late for Kimura, the reality of Slim's strategy. A captured Japanese intelligence officer later explained that they did not believe that there was more than one division in the area, and that it was directed down the west bank towards Yenangyaung.

This was a period of acute anxiety for Slim. The administrative risks he had taken now looked alarming. All but one (5th Indian Division) of his seven divisions and all but one of his five tank and independent brigades (the Lushai Brigade) was engaged. As the tempo increased, so too did Fourteenth Army's expenditure of petrol and ammunition, increasing the strain on the already stretched line of communication. 'Throughout the battle' he recorded, 'we were never without acute anxiety on the supply and transport side ... time and time again, and just in time, the bare essentials for their operations reached those who so critically needed them. Very rarely had any formation more than its basic needs.' His problems were compounded by the fact that on 23 February Chiang Kai-shek suddenly demanded the redeployment to China of all US and Chinese forces in the NCAC, and that US transport squadrons should fly them out. If Kimura withdrew the forces that he had facing the NCAC and threw them into the battle about Mandalay instead, at a time when Slim faced

A Vickers medium machine gun crew of the Indian Army guarding the flank of one of the bridging operations over the Irrawaddy, February 1945. (Victoria State Archives)

the loss of more of his precious aircraft, the challenge to Fourteenth Army would have been severe. But the threat was lifted in part by the US chiefs of staff agreeing, after representation from Mountbatten and the British chiefs of staff, to 'leave the bulk of their transport squadrons in Burma until either we had taken Rangoon or until 1 June, whichever was the earlier'. The prospect of recovering Rangoon by means of a land offensive – and thus the reopening of the old Burma Road – was slowly asserting itself in people's strategic consciousness.

Meanwhile, the decisive struggle for Meiktila was underway. Cowan advanced out of Nyaungu on 21 February. Despite having to cover difficult ground for tanks – the countryside was riven with deep, sandy gullies that required careful preparation to traverse – 17th Division and 255th Tank Brigade quickly captured Taungtha, the rear area for 33rd Division. The 17th Division then captured Kahlaing on 25 February, and on 26 February the airstrip at Thabutkon followed, exactly as planned. On news of its capture, 99th Brigade, waiting expectantly for this moment at Palel on the Imphal Plain, boarded their planes to fly in directly to the airfield, landing under enemy small-arms fire. Meanwhile, on 24 February, to reinforce Kimura's focus on Mandalay, 2nd Division crossed the Irrawaddy opposite the village of Ngazun, about 10 miles east of 20th Division's bridgehead at Myinmu. On 27 February, the vanguard of IV Corps had encircled Meiktila and was preparing to advance on the town from all directions. The Japanese commander of the Meiktila area, Major-General Tomekichi Kasuya, had some 12,000 troops as well as 1,500 miscellaneous base troops and hospital patients at his disposal for the defence of the town, and every man able to carry a weapon, wounded or otherwise, was pressed into service. Capturing Meiktila would not be easy. Strong positions were dug in covering a series of lakes to the west of the town. Routes into the town from the west and south were funnelled by the lakes, and easily covered by Japanese artillery fire. The Japanese, masters of the defence, rapidly turned buildings in the town into bunkers and strongpoints. Cowan decided to close the routes into the town, and attack directly from the north and east.

Troops of the 9th Battalion, the Border Regiment (the battalion in which the future author George Macdonald Fraser served as a lance-corporal) at Meiktila, February 1945. The battalion served as Motorized Infantry as part of 255th Tank Brigade. (Victoria State Archives)

Gurkha troops of the Indian Army approach Pagan, prior to forcing the crossing of the Irrawaddy, February 1945. (Victoria State Archives)

On the morning of 28 February he began to tighten the noose around the town. While 63rd Brigade brushed aside light opposition to move up closer to the town's western defences and placed a block with armour on the Chauk Road, 48th Brigade attacked from the north-east. Meanwhile, 255th Tank Brigade, with two infantry battalions and a self-propelled 105mm M7 'Priest' battery of 18th Field Regiment Royal Artillery under command, attacked east of Meiktila. Cowan's armour, deployed in wide-flanking aggressive actions, caught the Japanese defenders in the open and inflicted heavy casualties. The divisional artillery was concentrated, to enable it to fire missions in support of all points of the compass, and cab ranks of fighter-ground attack aircraft were established to do likewise from the air. With the jungle now behind them, 17th Indian Division's tanks, mechanized artillery and mechanized infantry found the flat lands beyond the Irrawaddy well suited to the tactics of encircling and cutting off Japanese positions. The Japanese had no answer to either Fourteenth Army's use of armour or to the effectiveness of the all-arms tactics in which it was employed. The attack penetrated well, but resistance was fierce and fanatical. Yet again, Japanese soldiers fought to the death, losing 5,000 dead and suffering 5,000 wounded in the battle for the town. Remarkably, 75 per cent of all Japanese defenders of Meiktila became casualties. Only 47 were taken prisoner, most of them in one of the captured hospitals, men unable to fight or kill themselves. By the end of the first day of the battle, Indian troops had penetrated well into the town. During 2 and 3 March, the 63rd, 48th and 255th Tank brigades closed in, squeezing and destroying the Japanese defenders between them. By 1800hrs on 3 March, Meiktila fell. During 4 and 5 March even the most fanatical resistance was brushed aside as surrounding villages were cleared and the main airfield secured.

Kimura was shocked, as Slim knew he would be, by the sudden and unexpected loss of Meiktila. The rapier thrust against his vulnerable rear, striking across the Irrawaddy far to the south, many miles from where his attention had been fixed by Slim's deception plan, was a profound surprise. He at once sought to crush 17th Indian Division and recapture the town. Kimura ordered Honda immediately to turn south, and for three weeks from mid-March the Japanese mounted a series of ferocious counter-attacks with six brigades, artillery and tanks against 17th Indian Division and 255th Tank Brigade. Isolated in Meiktila – 7th Indian Division had yet to clear the route from the Irrawaddy – Cowan's policy was one of 'aggressive defence'. Combined-arms groups of infantry, mechanized artillery and armour, supported from the air by attack aircraft, were sent out every day to hunt, ambush and destroy approaching Japanese columns in a radius of 20 miles of the town. The pressure on Meiktila built up, however. Soon the land line of communication back to Nyaungu was cut, and the Japanese threw everything they had at seizing the airfield. Aerial resupply was key to sustaining Messervy's troops in processes perfected the previous year in Arakan, Kohima and Imphal. The situation was sufficiently disconcerting for Slim to decide to commit his last remaining reserve, 5th Indian Division, one brigade of which (9th Brigade) arrived onto one of the Meiktila airfields, under enemy fire, on 17 March. This was a huge risk. But he knew that if he did not secure victory in this battle, he would have to concede the campaign. His gamble paid off. By 29 March the Japanese had been beaten back, losing their guns and significant casualties in the process. The river port of Myingyan on the Chindwin was captured after a fierce fight by 7th Indian Division, reinforced by one of the mechanized brigades from 5th Indian Division (Slim had moved its second armoured brigade north to support the advance of 19th Indian Division on Mandalay), and its rapid commissioning as a working port substantially reduced the

Gurkha troops of the Indian Army fighting through Pagan, February 1945. (Victoria State Archives)

pressure on Messervy's land line of communication. Before long, it was receiving 200 tons of desperately needed supplies every day. A few days later Taungtha was recaptured.

Slim's relief at the securing of the Meiktila battlefield was palpable, and he gave thanks where it was due. He was in no doubt that Cowan's success first in seizing Meiktila, then in holding the town against increasingly frantic Japanese counter-attacks, secured the success of Operation *Extended Capital*. The battle was, he reflected, 'a magnificent feat of arms [which] sealed the fate of the Japanese in Burma'. This was no over-statement. IV Corps' thrust against Meiktila was Slim's decisive stroke, on which the success of his entire strategy rested, and for which he had subordinated everything else. Now, the huge risks he had taken had come good. The Japanese also were in no doubt about the significance of Slim's victory, Kimura admitting that it was 'the masterpiece of Allied strategy' in the battle for Burma. The historian Louis Allen regarded it as 'Slim's greatest triumph', a feat which allowed him to place 'his hand firmly on the jugular of the Japanese' and which put 'the final reconquest of Burma within Slim's grasp'.

Slim now needed to attack Kimura hard in order to prevent him from turning against the IV Corps anvil forming around Meiktila. When this anvil was firm, Slim intended to allow XXXIII Corps – the hammer – to fall on Kimura hard from the north. The first part of this hammer – 19th Indian Division (62nd, 64th and 98th brigades) – broke out of its bridgehead 40 miles north of Mandalay on 26 February. By 4 March the division was in tankable country 20 miles north of Mandalay. The Japanese 15th and 33rd divisions had no answer to the pace of Rees' advance, nor to the attacks launched at them from the air. Aircraft – Beaufighter and Mosquito light

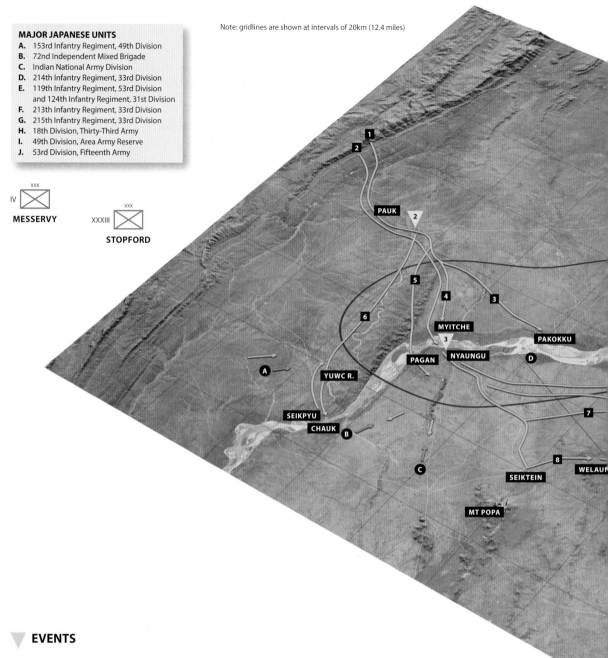

MAJOR JAPANESE UNITS

A. 153rd Infantry Regiment, 49th Division
B. 72nd Independent Mixed Brigade
C. Indian National Army Division
D. 214th Infantry Regiment, 33rd Division
E. 119th Infantry Regiment, 53rd Division
and 124th Infantry Regiment, 31st Division
F. 213th Infantry Regiment, 33rd Division
G. 215th Infantry Regiment, 33rd Division
H. 18th Division, Thirty-Third Army
I. 49th Division, Area Army Reserve
J. 53rd Division, Fifteenth Army

Note: gridlines are shown at intervals of 20km (12.4 miles)

IV ⊠ XXX
MESSERVY

XXXIII ⊠ XXX
STOPFORD

PAUK
MYITCHE
PAKOKKU
PAGAN
NYAUNGU
YUWC R.
SEIKPYU
CHAUK
SEIKTEIN
WELAU
MT POPA

▼ EVENTS

1. 20th Indian Division captures Monywa on 22 January. Lieutenant-General Slim establishes his Fourteenth Army HQ here on 8 February.

2. By 28 January the lead elements of IV Corps emerge through the track they have built for themselves through the Kabaw/Myittha Valley, arriving at Pauk, readying to cross the Irrawaddy in secret at Pakokku, Nyaungu and Pagan. The 28th East African Brigade are sent further south to Seikpyu as a diversion.

3. 7th Indian Division and 255th Tank Brigade arrive opposite Nyaungu and begin crossing on 14 February. Further north, 114th Indian Brigade launches a feint towards Pakokku, which is known to be strongly defended by the Japanese 214th Infantry Regiment. Meanwhile, XXXIII Corps is massing on the west bank of the Irrawaddy north of Mandalay, successfully persuading Kimura that this will be the point of Slim's main effort.

4. Lead elements of IV Corps (including 255th Tank Brigade) drive north-east parallel with the river to fall on Taungtha. They do not want to give away the secret just yet that the target is in fact Meiktila, to the south-east.

5. 7th Indian Division and 255th Tank Brigade then drive hard for Meiktila, brushing aside opposition, and reach Thabutkon on 26 February, where they are joined by the air-transported troops of 99th Indian Brigade. Together they advance on Meiktila, capturing it after a sharp fight on 5 March. Fierce Japanese counter-attacks are launched immediately, but to no avail.

6. Meanwhile, west of Mandalay 20th Indian Division and 2nd British Division build up forces along the Irrawaddy at Myinmu to give Kimura a sense that this would be the right flank of the Fourteenth Army advance (it was, in fact, far to the south). Crossings begin on 26 February. There is no rush to press forwards. The aim is a slow advance to draw in Japanese troops of 31st Division and prevent them turning to fall on the Fourteenth Army's strategic objective, Meiktila.

7. Meanwhile, the reinforced 19th Indian Division waits to cross the Irrawaddy in early March, building up its resources and attempting to persuade Kimura that this is the primary thrust. Once over the Irrawaddy, the division presses south towards Mandalay. The city is captured on 20 March.

8. Troops from 19th Division then progress south, where they are met by troops of 100th Indian Brigade advancing north along the railway, and 32nd Indian Brigade advancing from the west, on 29 and 30 March.

FOURTEENTH ARMY'S TRIUMPH: THE BATTLE FOR THE IRRAWADDY, FEBRUARY–MARCH 1945

The Irrawaddy River, stretching from Mandalay in the north-east to the village of Chauk on the east bank of the river in the south-west, was the scene of Lieutenant-General Slim's great triumph in February and March 1945. General Kimura had withdrawn his forces to the southern side of the river, protecting Mandalay. Slim judged, however, that Kimura's weakest point lay far to the south of Mandalay, and decided to feint in the north with XXXIII Corps but to strike hard in the south – anchored on the Japanese rear area at Meiktila, with the armoured and air-transportable IV Corps.

Burma Area ⊠ XXXX

KIMURA

N

SAW/MYITTHA VALLEY

MONYWA

CHINDWIN R.

MYINMU

IRRAWADDY R.

MYOTHA

AMARAPURA

MANDALAY

TAUNGTHA

KYAUKSE

PINDALE

BUTKON

MEIKTILA

WUNDWIN

RAILWAY

THAZI

MAJOR ALLIED UNITS

1. 7th Indian Division, IV Corps
2. 17th Indian Division, IV Corps and 255th Tank Brigade
3. 114th Indian Brigade, 7th Indian Division, IV Corps
4. 33rd Brigade, 7th Indian Division, IV Corps
5. 89th Brigade, 7th Indian Division, IV Corps
6. 28th East African Brigade, IV Corps
7. 48th Brigade, 17th Indian Division, IV Corps and 255th Tank Brigade
8. 63rd Brigade, 17th Indian Division, IV Corps
9. 5th Indian Division, IV Corps
10. Airlanding by 99th Indian Brigade, 17th Indian Division, IV Corps
11. Airlanding by 9th Indian Brigade, 5th Indian Division, IV Corps
12. 32nd Brigade, 20th Indian Division, IV Corps
13. 100th Brigade, 20th Indian Division, IV Corps
14. 80th Brigade, 20th Indian Division, IV Corps
15. 2nd British Division, XXXIII Indian Corps
16. 19th Indian Division, XXXIII Indian Corps

Japanese dead at Meiktila, March 1945. (Imperial War Museum)

bombers, together with the ubiquitous Hurribomber – coordinated their attacks with 19th Division's artillery, causing considerable damage to Japanese positions, while 19th Division and its mechanized reinforcements from 5th Division smashed through and around Japanese defences. The following day the Magyi Chaung, the last major physical obstacle in front of Mandalay, was breached and by 7 March the northern outskirts of Mandalay were reached. Kimura's dilemma was now palpable. He faced a decisive advance against his northern defences by 19th Indian Division; two full divisions were crossing the Irrawaddy west of the city at two separate points threatening to encircle Mandalay, and his critical administrative nerve centre at Meiktila was under heavy attack. Where should he reinforce? All were vital to him, but his choices were now impossible: reinforcing one vital area would entail reducing his strength at another.

The two strongpoints in Mandalay – Mandalay Hill and Fort Dufferin – were vigorously defended and required considerable effort to overcome. Allied troops entered the city on 9 March, but fierce fighting for the strongpoints meant that it wasn't captured until 20 March. True to form, the Japanese defenders fought to the last. Direct-fire artillery by 5.5in. howitzers and 2,000lb bombs dropped by Mitchell bombers were required to gain access to Fort Dufferin. On top of Mandalay Hill, the discovery that the Japanese had dug themselves into a warren of bunkers was solved by rolling lighted barrels of fuel into the tunnels. While Mandalay was being vested, 62nd Brigade struck secretly eastward at Maymyo where they fell upon the town, taking the garrison completely by surprise.

The second part of the XXXIII Corps advance – 20th Indian and British 2nd divisions – 40 and 25 miles west of Mandalay respectively, broke out of their bridgeheads in early March, touching each other on 2 March. The Japanese were everywhere pushed back, losing heavily in men and artillery. Slim deduced that Kimura would attempt to hold a line running south-west from Kyaukse to Chauk, with Fifteenth Army holding the right, Thirty-Third Army the centre, and Twenty-Eighth Army the left. He knew that despite Japanese efforts to stiffen the line, it would still be fragile. Accordingly, he aimed to concentrate at weak points in the line, and strike decisively at the Japanese command and communication network so as to remove the last vestiges of control Japanese commanders had over the course of the battle. Supported strongly by No. 221 Group RAF, Gracey's 20th Indian Division led the charge. The 32nd and 80th brigades sliced through the Japanese opposition to converge on Kyaukse, while 100th Brigade carried out a wide encircling movement to seize Wundin, on the main railway 60 miles south of Mandalay, on 21 March, although stubborn resistance prevented Kyaukse from falling until the end of the month. Throughout, Slim's aim was to keep the pressure on Kimura at every point of the compass. His planning cycle remained well ahead of Kimura's. 'No sooner was a plan made to meet a given situation than, due to a fresh move by Slim, it was out-of-date before it could be executed, and a new one had to be hurriedly prepared with a conglomeration of widely scattered units and formations,' observed Geoffrey Evans, reflecting from his position of intimate knowledge as GOC 7th Indian Division. 'Because of the kaleidoscopic changes in the situation, breakdowns in communication and the fact that Burma Area Army Headquarters was often out of touch with reality, many of the attacks to restore the position were uncoordinated.' The Japanese 15th and 31st divisions now retreated in disarray, breaking into little groups of fugitives seeking refuge in the Shan Hills to the east. Meanwhile, 2nd Division progressed methodically into Mandalay from the south-west, cutting the Ava–Mandalay road on 21 March and joining hands with 19th Indian Division. All around them, the men of Fourteenth Army saw a still-defiant though crumbling enemy. Pockets of desperate men continued to fight until destroyed in their bunkers and foxholes, burnt out by flame-throwers or destroyed by tanks and artillery in preference to sacrificing the infantry in assaults that did not justify the loss of Indian or British lives. By the end of the month the battle of the Irrawaddy shore had been won, the desperate remnants of the three divisions facing XXXIII Corps hurrying to escape through the hills to the east. Most Japanese divisions had lost between 30 and 50 per cent of their strength in casualties, with Fourteenth Army's battle casualties numbering 10,500. South of the city, at Meiktila, large swathes of the town and countryside lay in smoking ruins amid the dust and heat of high summer. Slim's great gamble had paid off. He now needed to see whether he could capitalize on this victory by seizing Rangoon 390 miles to the south – still an immense task – before the monsoon rains arrived again in all their fury.

ADVANCE IN ARAKAN

The onset of the monsoon in May 1944 had coincided with the successful conclusion of the campaign in the Mayu Range. With the demise of *Ha-Go* and the onset of *U-Go* in Manipur, offensive operations by the Allies in Arakan were paused until the start of the dry season in October. The threat to Chittagong had receded and the Japanese were now impossibly stretched. For Mountbatten, there was no strategic imperative to take any more ground in Arakan during the wet season other than making life as difficult

Arakan operations, 1944–45

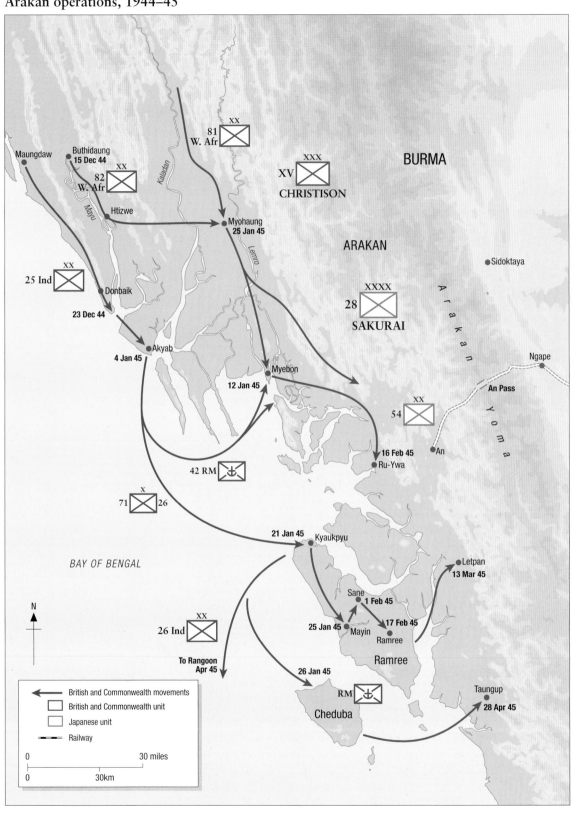

Maungdaw

Buthidaung
15 Dec 44

81
W. Afr

XX

82
W. Afr

XX

Htizwe

Kaladan

Myohaung
25 Jan 45

BURMA

XV
CHRISTISON

XXX

ARAKAN

Sidoktaya

25 Ind

XX

Donbaik

23 Dec 44

Lemro

28
SAKURAI

XXXX

Arakan

yoma

Ngape

Akyab

4 Jan 45

Myebon
12 Jan 45

An Pass

54

XX

16 Feb 45

An

Ru-Ywa

42 RM

71 **26**
X

21 Jan 45

Kyaukpyu

Letpan
13 Mar 45

BAY OF BENGAL

Sane
1 Feb 45

17 Feb 45

26 Ind

XX

25 Jan 45

Mayin

Ramree

N

To Rangoon
Apr 45

26 Jan 45

Ramree

RM

Cheduba

Taungup
28 Apr 45

British and Commonwealth movements
British and Commonwealth unit
Japanese unit
Railway

0   30 miles

0   30km

58

as possible for the Japanese. Lieutenant-General Sir Philip Christison's XV Corps held its position during one of the wettest monsoons on record, while Sakurai's weakened Twenty-Eighth Army adjusted itself to focus on defending Akyab and preparing for the inevitable Allied advance when the dry season returned. By the end of the fighting in Manipur in August 1944, and with Slim's plans for pursuit into Upper Burma, the strategic significance of Arakan reasserted itself. It provided a stepping stone by sea and air to Rangoon, and by land via the An Pass and Taungup into Central Burma. The XV Corps now comprised 25th and 26th Indian and 81st and 82nd West African divisions, together with 3 Commando Brigade, 22nd East African Brigade and 50th Tank Brigade, equipped with Sherman tanks.

While Mandalay was the primary focus of the Allied advance into Burma, there to face the concentrated might of Kimura's Burma Area Army, the need to secure Arakan remained a critical component of SEAC strategy. It would prevent the Japanese Twenty-Eighth Army in Arakan from providing

Indian troops clambering up a rough, precipitous hillside in typical Arakan hill country. (Keystone/Getty Images)

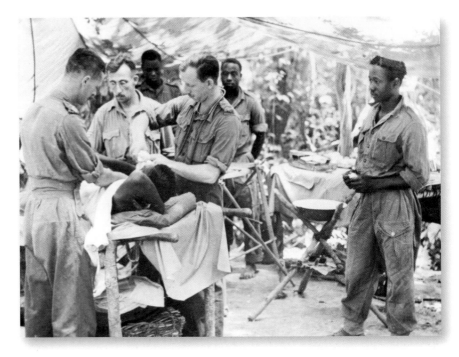

Doctors tend a wounded soldier of the 81st West African Division in an improvised operating theatre in the Kaladan Valley, August 1944. (Imperial War Museums via Getty Images)

support to Kimura's defence of Central Burma, and possession of the airfields at Akyab and at Kyaukpyu on Ramree Island would bring Rangoon into economical flying range of Allied transport aircraft. Akyab also offered a side door into Central Burma to support land operations against Rangoon when the advance began from Meiktila and Mandalay, once those battles had been successfully concluded. By then Fourteenth Army would have long outrun its logistic support from Imphal and Tamu and aerial resupply from Akyab would help fill that void. More importantly perhaps for Allied strategy was the opportunity the capture of Ramree and Cheduba offered for the amphibious attack on Rangoon – Operation *Dracula* – which was assumed by most in London and Washington to be the only way to take the capital before the beginning of the next monsoon season in May 1945. The arguments for mounting the assault in Arakan were presented by Mountbatten to the chiefs of staff against opposition from General Albert Wedemeyer, who had relieved Stilwell in Chungking, who worried that the operation would divert resources from China. But Mountbatten persisted. He argued that operations to defeat Sakurai in Arakan were designed to do precisely what Slim was in the process of doing in Upper and Central Burma, namely, to push out the Japanese and so open up the new Burma Road. Defeating the Japanese in Burma was the best way of ensuring China remained supplied, and engaged in the fight. Even doubling or tripling the resources available to China (instead of devoting them to operations *Capital* and *Dracula*) would do nothing to defeat Kimura, and until he was defeated, the Japanese would retain control of Central Burma. The irony was that it was Fourteenth Army – supported by XV Corps in Arakan – that was now in the process of spectacularly achieving what the Americans had long demanded of the British in Burma, although Wedemeyer's US-tinted political spectacles meant that he still couldn't quite see it.

In the event, XV Corps' advance down the coastline when it began in December 1944 – Operation *Romulus* – went far better than planned,

Sakurai pulling back before the pressure, despite fierce local resistance. The 82nd West African Division had already reoccupied Buthidaung, allowing Major-General George Wood's 25th Indian Division to advance with 74th Brigade along the coast supplied by sea. A second brigade – the 53rd – advanced on the eastern side of the Mayu Range, also supported by a river line of communication on the Mayu and Kalapanzin rivers. The focus for both brigades was 'fighting forward', rather than looking back to the road behind them. The advancing battalions coordinated their march with integrated armour, artillery and fighter ground attack, bypassing opposition and allowing centres of resistance to be dealt with by troops following up behind. The confidence of the army had been transformed. Despite the fury of the opposition they encountered, the troops of XV Corps now had an answer to every tactical problem they faced. In the language of the time, their tails were up. Their focus on the strategic imperative – the capture of Akyab – meant that they had no reason to be distracted by opposition which they deemed to be strategically insignificant. They ignored repeated Japanese attempts at encirclement and infiltration, driving forward to their objective and shrugging off attempts by the Japanese to divert them from this course.

A new and dramatic dimension to *Romulus* was the flanking march down the remote and roadless Kaladan Valley by Major-General Frederick Loftus-Tottenham's 81st West African Division. The Kaladan River drains into the sea at Akyab. The West Africans, advancing down the roadless valley, were supplied by air for nine months, operating behind what would conventionally be described as 'the front line'. Combat operations in the Kaladan Valley,

Indian Army soldiers wade ashore at Akyab (modern Sittwe), in January 1945. (Universal Images Group via Getty Images)

General Kodendera Subayya Thimayya in a post-war photograph. Thimayya was the only Indian to command an infantry brigade in battle during the war, and later became the Indian Chief of Army Staff. (KEYSTONE-FRANCE/Gamma-Rapho via Getty Images)

though significant, were less important to Christison than the pressure this move placed on Sakurai, who now had two fronts to watch. This exercise in long-range penetration was an effective use of the concept, but, like the work of the Lushai Brigade in holding the right flank of the Chin Hills during the advance to the Chindwin, and in contrast to the much better-known Operation *Thursday*, is little known. There was no fanfare about its work at the time. No war correspondents accompanied its long march into Japanese-held territory and few visitors arrived to acknowledge the extraordinary work of these volunteer soldiers from Nigeria, the Gold Coast (the Gambia) and Sierra Leone, few of whom had been soldiers before the divisions had been raised in Africa in 1943.

On the coast, Foul Point was reached on Boxing Day two weeks earlier than expected and preparations were made for the assault on Akyab. This was a task allocated to 3 Commando Brigade, the two Royal Marine and two Army commandos (about 500 men each), recently arrived from Europe, which were itching for a fight. In the air No. 224 Group and at sea Force W and a powerful naval bombardment group (Task Force 61, comprising HMSs *Queen Elizabeth* – which hadn't fired its 15in. guns in anger since Gallipoli in 1915 – *Newcastle*, *Nigeria* and *Kenya*, HMAS *Napier*, *Nepal* and *Norman*, and two other fleet destroyers, the escort carrier HMS *Ameer*, and 20 other vessels) prepared to support the first amphibious landings in theatre. In the event, Sakurai evacuated the town and it was taken without firing a shot. Sakurai had been forced to use two of the three battalions guarding the town to counter the advance to his rear right flank by the West Africans, who had captured the key ferry at Kyawktaw on Christmas Day. Realizing that he could no longer defend Akyab with the forces at his disposal, he withdrew to defend the route into Burma proper through the hill tracks via Taungup, 130 miles to the south. The strategic effect of the Kaladan Valley operation, in terms of the influence it had on achieving Christison's overall strategic objective in Arakan – the capture of Akyab – was enormous. By forcing Sakurai to withdraw from Akyab, a battle that would have consumed considerable time, scarce material and lives, it was 81st West African Division that won the battle for the town. It was a classic example of the power of manoeuvre – rather than the bludgeoning tactics deployed by Irwin in 1943 – that forced the issue for Sakurai, obliging him to conform to Mountbatten's plan.

The initiative now lay with Christison. In order to stop Sakurai from withdrawing in good order into Central Burma, Christison needed to capture the town of Kangaw. This would also prevent Sakurai from counter-attacking the planned offensive by 81st West African Division against Myohaung,

the ancient capital of Arakan that lay at the mouth of the Kaladan River. Christison used his amphibious capability to cut the coast road. 3 Commando Brigade, whose amphibious assault against Myebon through a maze of outlying mangrove swamps on 12 January 1945 was coordinated with close air support and a naval bombardment, succeeded in forming a bridgehead, through which the all-Indian 51st Infantry Brigade of 25th Indian Division was inserted from the sea. This brigade was commanded by the Sandhurst-trained Lieutenant-Colonel Kodendera Subayya ('Timmy') Thimayya. The Japanese, reacting strongly against this threat to their rear, struck back in a series of savage counter-attacks, but failed to dislodge the beachhead. Following the Commandos came artillery and a troop of Sherman tanks of 19th Lancers.

To clear the Japanese from the Myebon Peninsula required their removal from the village of Kangaw, overlooked by a point denoted on Allied maps as Hill 170, where the roads in the area came together. It was to prove to be one of the most vicious battles of the entire war. After a week of fighting Japanese attempts to push the intruders back into the sea failed, and the commandos fought to capture Kangaw Village and occupy Hill 170 on 29 January. The Japanese then did what they did best, throwing repeated and suicidal waves of assaults against the entrenched defenders. The Japanese attacks were mounted with considerable skill, accompanied by significant artillery bombardment and supporting machine-gun fire. The terrible hand-to-hand struggles that took place typified the horror of this war, with a significant resonance of Kohima, but it was an unequal struggle for the Japanese. By 3 February it was all over, Japanese bodies in places stacked in piles on top

Lieutenant M.H. Jerram, Royal Indian Navy Volunteer Reserve (left) with the gun crew of the Indian sloop *Narbada* at Myebon. The gun barrels were blistered during the bombardment of the Arakan coast. (Imperial War Museums via Getty Images)

LIEUTENANT GEORGE KNOWLAND VC, ARAKAN, JANUARY 1945 (PP. 64–65)

On 31 January 1945, near Kangaw in Arakan, Lieutenant George Knowland of 3 Commando Brigade was commanding the forward platoon of a troop positioned on the extreme north of a hill known as Hill 170, which was subjected to very heavy and repeated Japanese attacks throughout the day. Before the first attack started, Lieutenant Knowland's platoon was heavily mortared and machine-gunned, yet he moved about among his men keeping them alert and encouraging them, though under fire himself at the time.

When the enemy, some 300 strong in all, made their first assault, they concentrated all their efforts on his platoon of 24 men; but in spite of the ferocity of the attack, Knowland moved about from trench to trench distributing ammunition, and firing his rifle and throwing grenades at the enemy, often from completely exposed positions.

Later, when the crew of one of his forward Bren guns had all been wounded, Knowland (**1**) sent back to troop headquarters for another crew and ran forward to man the gun himself until they arrived. The Japanese (**2**) were then fewer than 10 yards from him in dead ground down the hill, so in order to get a better field of fire, he stood on top of the trench, firing the light machine gun from his hip and successfully keeping them at a distance until a medical orderly had dressed and evacuated the wounded men behind him. The new Bren Gun team also became casualties on the way up and Lieutenant Knowland continued to fire the gun until another team took over.

Later, when a fresh attack came in, he took over a 2in. mortar, and in spite of heavy fire and the closeness of the enemy, he stood up in the open to face them, firing the mortar from his hip and killing six of them with his first bomb. When all bombs were expended, he went back through heavy grenade, mortar and machine-gun fire to get more, which he fired in the same way from the open in front of his platoon positions. When those bombs were finished, he went back to his own trench, and still standing up fired his rifle at them. Being hard pressed and with the enemy closing in on him from only 10 yards away, he had no time to recharge his magazine. Snatching up the Tommy gun of a casualty, he sprayed the enemy and was mortally wounded stemming this assault, though not before he had killed and wounded many of the enemy.

Such was the inspiration of Knowland's magnificent heroism, that, though 14 out of 24 of his platoon became casualties at an early stage, and six of his positions were over-run by the enemy, his men held on through 12 hours of continuous and fierce fighting until reinforcements arrived. If this northern end of the hill had fallen, the rest of the hill would have been endangered, the beachhead dominated by the enemy and other units farther inland cut off from their source of supplies. As it was, the final successful counter-attack was later launched from the vital ground which Lieutenant Knowland had played such a gallant part in holding.

RAF aircrews preparing bombs at a forward base in Burma, February 1945. (Imperial War Museum)

of each other on the slopes of Hill 170. It was estimated that 2,500 died in this last-ditch attempt to delay the inevitable. Allied casualties – some 500 – were also high. Two Victoria Crosses were awarded in this single battle, 'Timmy' Thimayya receiving both the DSO and a Mention in Despatches. 3 Commando Brigade were astonished at the fighting proficiency of the Indian troops alongside whom they fought. Their commander, Brigadier Campbell Hardy, who had 8th/19th Hyderabad under command for a short period during the battle, presented the battalion with a green beret, the only item they had readily to hand, with a typed message on a card: 'We cannot buy anything here but we would like you to accept this as a token of our great admiration for the bravery and achievement of your battalion.' Success at Kangaw was crowned by the capture of Myohaung by the West Africans. Caught between two pincers the remnants of the Japanese 54th Division broke and began to stream across the mountains to the east, through An and Taungup.

The primary military task remaining in Arakan after these victories was to capture Ramree and Cheduba islands, completed at the end of February 1945. The 15in. guns of HMS *Queen Elizabeth* covered the successful landing by 26th Indian Division. It was an unequal task, 980 of the Japanese garrison of 1,000 dying before the island fell. At no time did Sakurai appear to realize the strategic significance of these airfields to Allied plans, dissipating what combat effort he had in suicidal missions seemingly disconnected to each other.

For the Allies, Rangoon was now in reach of bombers, as was Central Burma, in time to help sustain the advance southwards of Fourteenth Army. More importantly, an advanced base for Operation *Dracula* had been secured. Hard fighting characterized the short campaign between December 1944 and February 1945, but the overwhelming weight of operational ability, tactical skill, manpower and materiel provided a stark difference to the First Arakan campaign two years – and seemingly several light years – before.

THE RACE FOR RANGOON

SEAC now faced its final and arguably greatest challenge: to capture Rangoon before the monsoon rains in May made such a proposition by land impossible. The rapid advance by Fourteenth Army into Upper Burma since the previous December had led Mountbatten to suggest to London in February that Operation *Dracula* would no longer be required, given the progress of Slim's operations on the Irrawaddy and Christison's in Arakan. In March, however, Slim was not so sure. Kimura had been defeated on the Irrawaddy, but capturing a well-defended Rangoon would be an immense and complex operation.

Rangoon was over 390-miles further on from Mandalay, where the logistics stretch was already being felt by troops in the vanguard of the fighting. Food, fuel and ammunition were all rationed; every bullet, artillery shell, gallon of petrol and tin of bully beef had either to be brought along the tortuous line of communication – a single road – from Dimapur, or flown from the airfields in Assam and Tripura directly to the battle area. A further push by even half of his army – such as the mechanized IV Corps – would add intolerable pressure on his logistics system, which was already running at maximum capacity. Some pressure on the delivery of fuel had been alleviated by the completion of a pipeline from Dimapur to Imphal and on to Tamu, in its own right a remarkable civil engineering achievement. This reduced the requirement to carry fuel forward in 44-gallon drums in the holds of the precious transport aircraft, which in the days of ubiquitous smoking was a safety nightmare. If the fragile resupply structure failed before IV Corps had even reached Rangoon, Slim's plan to smash Japanese resistance across the whole of Burma would also fail. If the Japanese were intent on defending Rangoon with anything like the intelligence and tenacity that had

A Sherman of 255th Tank Brigade, part of IV Corps, at the village of Pyinbongyi on the road to Rangoon, May 1945. (Imperial War Museum)

marked their defensive operations elsewhere in the campaign, Slim did not want his tactical choices determined by lack of fuel, food or ammunition. Failure at the gates of Rangoon for 'want of a nail' was not something he could contemplate.

With *Dracula* now off, SEAC planning staff were busy working on another amphibious option, to land a newly constructed XXXIV Corps (23rd Indian Division, 81st West African Division and 3 Commando Brigade) on the coast of Thailand in preparation for an overland advance towards Singapore. But when Slim voiced his concerns about Rangoon to Mountbatten, the Supremo immediately saw their sense and on 2 April turned planning for *Dracula* back on. In an indication of just how quickly SEAC could operate by 1945, the date for the planned divisional-sized airborne and amphibious assault on Rangoon was set for four weeks hence, 5 May 1945.

If the strategic challenge was the capture of Rangoon before the monsoon broke by means of a two-pronged attack, one from the land and the other by sea and air (i.e. parachute), Slim's operational challenge was to divide his army between a component that

A Karen resistance fighter, working with SOE. (Victoria State Archives)

could get there in a month, defeating a formidable enemy on the way, and a component that could defeat the still-dangerous remnants of Kimura's army that had been pushed into the eastern hills. The defeat of the Japanese on the Irrawaddy did not mean for one moment that they were now without fight. Far from it. They could still put up a savage resistance at multiple points across southern and eastern Burma that held the possibility of a grinding campaign akin to the desperately bloody battles that characterized the fighting across the Pacific. Slim had originally envisaged both of his corps advancing on Rangoon in a reversal of General Shojiro Iida's 1942 offensive, one corps using the Irrawaddy and the other moving down the general route of the Meiktila–Rangoon railway. Even though it meant dividing his forces, a double advance would, Slim considered, provide Kimura with the same option of difficulties that he had been faced with at Mandalay, and which had challenged Slim back in 1942. But the impossibility of sustaining two separate corps with the limited logistical resources at his disposal meant that he only had enough for a single corps' advance on Rangoon, along the railway axis through Toungoo and Pegu. In any case, Slim needed speed, to cut off Twenty-Eighth Army in the south, preventing it from reinforcing Rangoon or retreating across the Sittang. The plan on which he determined was for Messervy's corps at Meiktila to strike for Rangoon, punching south while avoiding direct fights, bypassing significant pockets of enemy resistance, all the while being resupplied by air. Meanwhile, XXXIII Corps would methodically clear Japanese from the Yenangyaung oilfields, before pushing down the Irrawaddy to Prome. To allow IV Corps to

ATTACK ON PYINBONGYI, APRIL 1945 (PP. 70–71)

This all-arms assault by the men of 63rd Indian Brigade (**1**), part of 17th Indian Division and IV Indian Corps, captures the essence of the Indian Army in its triumphant sweep 400 miles from Meiktila to Rangoon in the pre-monsoon period of 1945. Now only 68 miles from Rangoon, IV Corps is moving quickly down the road and rail route to the capital city, clearing enemy-held villages and pushing aside repeated roadblocks using all-arms fire and movement. Artillery would fire on the enemy position while tanks, mechanized infantry and combat engineers would attempt to push around the enemy positions, leaving the 'mopping up' to a by now thoroughly synchronized assault by tanks, infantry and aircraft.

The Sherman tanks (**2**) had only arrived in theatre at the end of 1944, but the whole of IV Indian Corps was by now very slick in combat operations combining tanks, infantry, self-propelled 105mm guns ('Priests'), Combat Air Support by Hurribombers and Thunderbolts, and combat engineers repairing bridges, disposing of mines and obstacles along the path of the advance. A 'cab rank' of close air support aircraft (**3**) would remain permanently above the advancing troops during the hours of daylight, allowing for their immediate use when required to assist in the ground attack. Auster light aircraft would also be airborne, spotting targets for the artillery moving up on tracks below. When required, Liberator bombers from the RAF and USAAF would also target defended positions in advance of an attack by ground forces.

The 63rd Indian Infantry Brigade had been formed at Jhansi in January 1942: it spent most of the war as part of the famous 17th Indian Division commanded by Major General D.T. 'Punch' Cowan. In April 1945 it comprised 7th/10th Baluch Regiment, 1st/10th Gurkha Rifles and the 9th Battalion, the Border Regiment. The experiences of the latter battalion are memorably described by George Macdonald Fraser in *Quartered Safe Out Here*. The brigade reached an evacuated Rangoon on 3 May 1945, the enemy fleeing eastwards across the Sittang.

SOE operations in Burma, 1944–45

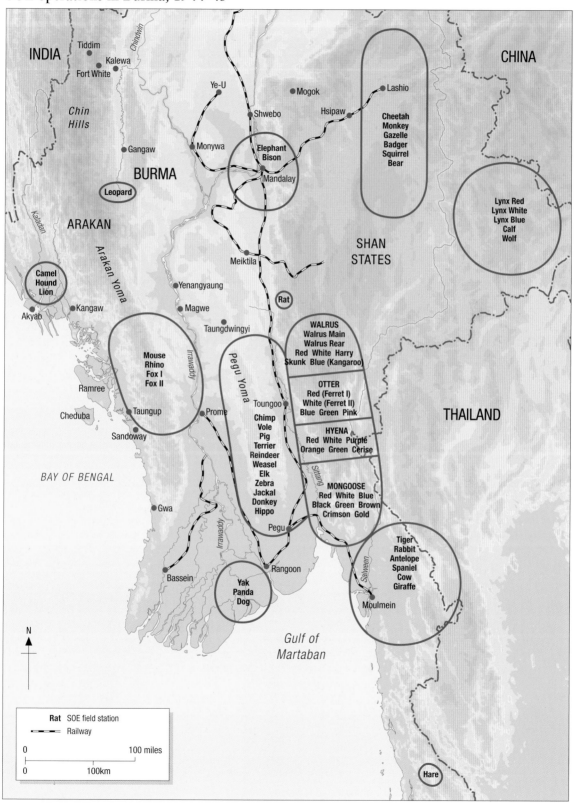

INDIA

Tiddim

Kalewa

Fort White

Chin Hills

Gangaw

BURMA

ARAKAN

Arakan Yoma

Kaladan

Akyab

Kangaw

Ramree

Cheduba

Sandoway

Taungup

Irrawaddy

BAY OF BENGAL

Gwa

Bassein

Ye-U

Shwebo

Monywa

Mandalay

Meiktila

Yenangyaung

Magwe

Taungdwingyi

Prome

Toungoo

Pegu

Pegu Yoma

Irrawaddy

Rangoon

Mogok

Hsipaw

Lashio

SHAN STATES

THAILAND

CHINA

Sittang

Salween

Moulmein

Gulf of Martaban

Leopard

Camel Hound Lion

Rat

Elephant Bison

Cheetah Monkey Gazelle Badger Squirrel Bear

Lynx Red Lynx White Lynx Blue Calf Wolf

Mouse Rhino Fox I Fox II

WALRUS Walrus Main Walrus Rear Red White Harry Skunk Blue (Kangaroo)

OTTER Red (Ferret I) White (Ferret II) Blue Green Pink

HYENA Red White Purple Orange Green Cerise

MONGOOSE Red White Blue Black Green Brown Crimson Gold

Chimp Vole Pig Terrier Reindeer Weasel Elk Zebra Jackal Donkey Hippo

Tiger Rabbit Antelope Spaniel Cow Giraffe

Yak Panda Dog

Hare

N

Rat	SOE field station
▬▬▬	Railway

0   100 miles

0   100km

sustain its southward advance, a further restructuring of the aerial resupply arrangements to Fourteenth Army were put in place. The whole of IV Corps was placed on aerial resupply, together with one division of XXXIII Corps. The remainder of XXXIII Corps was to rely on rail, river and road transport, maximizing use of the considerable river flotilla that had been built at Kalewa the previous December and which was now operating out of the Irrawaddy river port Myingyan. Christison's success in securing Akyab and Ramee greatly facilitated the advance to Rangoon because of the access to Arakanese airfields. The advance to Rangoon was to be undertaken by five divisions of the Indian Army; the two British divisions – the 36th and 2nd – were sent back to India, in part because the logistical requirements for sustaining Indian divisions by air supply were considerably less than those of the British.

A significant new feature of the fighting in Burma in 1945 was the work of irregular forces inside Burma in support of Fourteenth Army operations. After the retreat to India in 1942 little immediate effort had been made to retain contact with those of the hill tribes in the north and east of the country – the Kachins, Shans and Karens respectively – who would be interested in continuing resistance to the Japanese during the occupation and might be willing to support more conventional operations if and when a reconquest of Burma became possible. In 1942, Karen members of the Burma Rifles had been sent home with their weapons and urged to await the return of the British. Unable to make his own escape, one officer – Major Hugh Seagrim – remained with the Karens, although because of his lack of a radio, contact wasn't made with him by India Command until October 1943. When an SOE team finally reached him, he reported that the Karens were awaiting their liberation and would be prepared to help fight for it. The Japanese, however, had got wind of Seagrim's presence and in a ruthless campaign against the Karens forced him to surrender. He was executed in Rangoon in September 1944.

Nevertheless, the potential of a Karenni-based resistance raised the possibility, long argued by old Burma hands, of a British armed and trained fifth column operating behind Japanese lines for the purpose of gathering battlefield intelligence and undertaking limited guerrilla action of the type that had developed in occupied Europe. Slim had long complained about the poor quality of the battlefield intelligence (as opposed to signals intelligence, about which he was well provided) that he and his corps commanders received. He was concerned, among other things, about knowing 'what was on the other side of the hill', the product of information provided – where it existed – by effective combat (ground and air) reconnaissance. There was no shortage of organizations attempting to assist in this task – at least 12 – but their coordination was poor and most reported to SEAC or parts of India Command, rather than to Fourteenth Army. Slim dismissed most of these as 'private armies' which offered no real help to the task of defeating the enemy on the battlefield.

One of the groups, part of Force 136 (i.e. Special Operations Executive, or SOE), which had operated in front of 20th Indian Division along the Chindwin between 1943 and early 1944 under Major Edgar Peacock (and thus known as 'P Force') did sterling work with local Burmese and Karen agents reporting on Japanese activity facing IV Corps. Persuaded that similar groups working among the Karens in Burma's eastern hills – an area known as the Karenni States – could achieve significant support for a land offensive in Burma, Slim (to whom Mountbatten transferred responsibility for Force 136 in late 1944 for this purpose) authorized an operation to the Karens. Its task was not merely to undertake intelligence missions watching the roads and railways between Mandalay and Rangoon, but to determine whether the Karens would fight. If they were prepared

Kachin tribesmen from northern Burma wait in ambush in the jungle. The Kachin had joined forces with the Allies and caused heavy casualties among the Japanese due to their superior knowledge of the local terrain. (Keystone/Hulton Archive/Getty Images)

AMBUSH ON THE MAWCHI ROAD, KARENNI HILLS, APRIL 1945 (PP. 76–77)

Soldiers of Force 136 (SOE, **1**), together with the Karen guerrillas they have trained (**2**), ambush a Japanese convoy (**3**) en route along the road from Mawchi to Toungoo in April 1945. In one of the most critical operations of the war, 12,000 Karens, under the command of 210 men of Force 136, undertook a series of small-scale but crucial actions across 7,000 square miles of the Karenni (the Karen Hills) designed to prevent the Japanese from reinforcing the town of Toungoo.

Sited strategically on the Sittang, Toungoo was the key to winning the war for the Fourteenth Army before the monsoon rains arrived in May. If Slim could capture the town before the Japanese had a chance to reinforce it, he would be able to push his armoured vanguard (IV Indian Corps) on to Rangoon and potentially force the Japanese to evacuate the capital city before the Japanese were cut off from their escape route into Thailand. Weeks of ambushes and small-scale actions across the Karenni prevented the Japanese from reaching Toungoo and forced the Japanese to evacuate Rangoon, just before the amphibious Operation *Dracula* was launched against Rangoon from the sea.

The British had been slowly establishing their position among the Karens during late 1943 and through 1944, building on the legacy of Major Hugh Seagrim GC who had stayed in the hills ever since the Japanese invasion in 1942. Building up the Karen forces was a fundamental part of Slim's concept of battle, which entailed using special forces, such as Force 136, to complement his conventional forces, where it made sense to do so. Some 3,000 weapons were dropped by parachute to equip the force. Not only did Force 136 succeed in stopping the Japanese from securing Toungoo, but with their Bren guns, rifles and grenades the Karen guerrillas killed 11,874 Japanese, more than the IV Indian Corps. It was the perfect relationship between the fast armoured drive down the valley towards Toungoo, and the guerrilla effort in the hills, that made Slim's drive to Rangoon such a success and doomed the Japanese to destruction.

to do so, SOE would be responsible for training and organizing them as armed groups able to deliver battlefield intelligence directly in support of the advancing Fourteenth Army. The resulting operation – *Character* – was so spectacularly successful it outweighed what had been achieved by Operation *Thursday* the previous year in terms of its impact on the course of military operations to defeat the Japanese in Burma. It has been strangely forgotten, or ignored, by most historians ever since, drowned out perhaps by the noise made by the drama and heroism of Operation *Thursday*. Over the course of Operation *Extended Capital* some 2,000 British, Indian and Burmese officers and soldiers, along with 1,430 tons of supplies, were dropped into Burma for the purpose of providing intelligence about the Japanese that would be useful for the fighting formations of Fourteenth Army, as well as undertaking limited guerrilla operations. As historian Richard Duckett has observed, this found SOE operating not merely as intelligence gatherers in the traditional sense, but as Special Forces with a defined military mission fully integrated into Slim's overall battle plan. For Operation *Character* specifically, about 110 British officers and NCOs and over 100 men of all Burmese ethnicities, dominated interestingly by Burmans (by now also including three-man Jedburgh Teams) mobilized as many as 12,000 Karens over an area of 7,000 square miles to the anti-Japanese cause. Some 3,000 weapons were dropped into the Karenni States. Operating in four distinct groups ('Walrus', 'Otter', 'Hyena' and 'Mongoose') the Karen irregulars trained and led by Force 136, waited for the moment when Fourteenth Army instructed them to attack.

The earlier Force 136 operation to the AFO and BNA – *Nation* – had reaped its reward, with several thousand AFO guerrillas by the end of April operating under Jedburgh teams near Toungoo, the Sittang and Irrawaddy valley and delta, preparing to assist Operation *Dracula*. As many as 800 Japanese had been killed. General Aung San had, in a remarkable piece of theatre, paraded his army before General Kimura on the Padang in Rangoon on 27 March, before marching them away 'to engage with the British'. What

A British 3in. mortar detachment supports the 19th Indian Division's advance along the Mawchi Road east of Toungoo in April 1945. (Imperial War Museum)

none of the Japanese knew was that by this Aung San meant that he was about to turn his army of 7,000 over to the British, and fight against their erstwhile colleagues.

Despite his failure at Mandalay and Meiktila, Kimura was far from defeated. Although his attempt to defend Southern Burma by holding Slim at bay along the Irrawaddy had been a miserable failure, his divisions were still capable of fighting to a coherent plan and savagely contesting every inch of ground. The whole of Fourteenth Army knew that the Japanese, even when other armies would consider themselves beaten, would fight ferociously until death. The experience of the previous year, with 5th Indian Division advancing down the Tiddim Road and 11th East African Division pushing slowly down the Kabaw Valley, testified to their tenacious determination to trade every inch of territory as expensively as they could. But strangely, in a mirror of the failed British efforts to stem the victorious Japanese advance through Burma in 1942 – by building largely fictitious defensive 'lines' on a map rather than by creating a defence in depth – Kimura now attempted the same, ordering his troops to reform on a line from Yenangyaung on the Irrawaddy through to Pyawbwe, south of Meiktila, in the east. Sakurai's Twenty-Eighth Army and its two divisions, together with remnants of the INA, would hold the Irrawaddy at Yenangyaung (and hence access to Burma from Arakan) while Honda's Thirty-Third Army and its three divisions would hold the eastern pivot of this line at Pyawbwe, an otherwise insignificant village that nevertheless straddled the road and railway south to Toungoo. What was left of Katamura's mangled Fifteenth Army would be reconstituted as Kimura's reserve.

Between 30 March and 10 April 1945, Pyawbwe saw the first battle of Fourteenth Army's drive to Rangoon, and it proved as decisive in 1945 as the Japanese attack on Prome had been in 1942. Otherwise strong Japanese defensive positions around the town with limited capability for counter-attack meant that the Japanese were sitting targets for Allied tanks, artillery and air power. Messervy's plan was simple: to bypass the defended points that lay before Pyawbwe, allowing them to be dealt with by subsequent

Indian troops of 6th/7th Rajput Rifles moving through Pyawbwe north of Rangoon, May 1945. (AFP via Getty Images)

attack from the air, and surround Pyawbwe from all points of the compass with Major-General 'Punch' Cowan's 17th Indian Division before squeezing it like a lemon with his tanks and artillery. With nowhere to go, and with no effective counter-attack potential, the Japanese were exterminated bunker by bunker by the Shermans of 255th Tank Brigade, now slick with the experience of battle gained at Meiktila. Infantry, armour and aircraft cleared Honda's primary blocking point before Toungoo with coordinated precision. This single battle, which killed over 1,000 Japanese, entirely removed

Indian troops overrun a Japanese position along a road en route to Toungoo, April 1945. (Victoria State Archives)

Honda's ability to prevent IV Corps from exploiting the road to Toungoo. Messervy grasped the opportunity, leapfrogging 5th Indian Division (the vanguard of the advance comprising an armoured regiment and armoured reconnaissance group from 255th Tank Brigade, now commanded by Major-General Robert Mansergh) southwards, capturing Shwemyo on 16 April, Pyinmana on 19 April and Lewe on 21 April. Toungoo was the immediate target, attractive because it boasted three airfields, from where No. 224 Group could provide air support to Operation *Dracula*. Messervy drove his armour on, reaching Toungoo, much to the surprise of the Japanese, the following day. The 5th Indian Division had advanced 211 miles in 14 days, reaching Toungoo three days before even the most optimistic forecasts. After three days of fighting, supported by heavy attack from the air by B-24 Liberators, the town and its airfields fell to Messervy. On the very day of its capture, 100 C-47s and C-46 Commando transports landed the air-transportable elements of 17th Indian Division to join their armoured comrades. They now took the lead from 5th Indian Division, accompanied by 255th Tank Brigade, for whom rations in their supporting vehicles had been substituted for petrol, pressing on via Pegu to Rangoon.

The bold attack in depth that IV Corps' advance represented, the tip of Fourteenth Army's spear, was remarkable. Armour, infantry and tracked artillery worked in combined teams with intimate support provided in the air by continuous fighter-ground attack patrols linked by radio to the leading tanks. Each stage of the attack was undertaken to confuse Kimura; to act before he could respond to the previous threat, resulting in the Burma Area Army remaining in a state of command confusion for much of 1945. The single operational objective – to get to Rangoon before the rains fell – was prioritized before all else. Aerial resupply was a strategic function of SEAC, organized by Mountbatten in a single Air and Ground Supply Committee in March 1945 that prioritized air transport strictly in accordance with strategic priorities across the whole theatre. An additional strategic consideration needs to be recalled. Slim recognized that if the Japanese were able to hold Toungoo, and thus prevent Fourteenth Army making its way beyond this point, Kimura would not need to evacuate Rangoon. If Rangoon were defended, Operation *Dracula* would be opposed, with serious consequences

Consolidated Liberator B Mark VIs of No. 99 Squadron RAF, with their attendant ground crews, lined up at Dhubalia, India, preparing for a bombing raid over Burma. (Victoria State Archives)

in terms of casualties. Defeating the Japanese at Toungoo would, it was hoped, force Kimura to evacuate Rangoon beyond the Sittang to avoid being caught in a Fourteenth Army/Operation *Dracula* pincer.

The contribution of Operation *Character* to the advance by IV Corps to Toungoo and beyond was battle-winning. By April 1945 the Karen irregulars harried the 50,000 Japanese in the hills and directed air strikes, providing close reconnaissance of targets for No. 224 Group's aircraft. Their attacks, beginning in early April, were coordinated by HQ Fourteenth Army to coincide with the advance of elements of IV Corps, and were focused on preventing the Japanese 18th Division from reaching and reinforcing Toungoo before the arrival of 5th Indian Division. To get to Toungoo, 18th Division had to pass through areas of jungle hills to the north-east and east entirely dominated by Force 136. By means of repeated ambushes the Japanese were fought every step of the way. Large amounts of detailed target information was radioed through for use in attacks by the air force. The official historian of SOE observed 'that in the week before the fall of Rangoon (2 May 1945) almost all their long-range fighter-bombers were employed on Force 136 targets, and that so many high-grade reports came in that it was impossible to act on them all'. There were many notable successes, the principal being an attack on the railway station at Pyu which coincided with the arrival of a troop train, causing over 1,000 casualties. No. 221 Group RAF was so impressed with Force 136's later intelligence that they proposed that when operations began in Malaya, at least one squadron should stand by to carry out immediate strikes when a mobile target was reported – something that had not been done in Burma. Roadblocks, ambushes and demolitions held up the Japanese 18th Division's cross-country advance to Toungoo in the area of Mawchi, 50 miles east of Toungoo. In his immediate report on operations Slim described the operational effect of the Karen irregulars:

Our own levies led by their British officers were a most valuable asset and had a real influence on operations. They were tactically controlled by wireless from Army Headquarters, told when to rise, the objectives they should attack, and given specific tasks. They could not and were not expected to stand up to the Japanese in pitched battles but they could and did in places harry them unmercifully. Their greatest achievement was the delaying of 15th Japanese Division in the Loikaw–Mawchi area, thus enabling IV Corps to reach Toungoo first, but they have rendered almost equally valuable services. They had an excellent jitter effect on the Japanese, who were compelled to lock up troops to guard against attacks on the lines of communication.

The work of Force 136, in particular in operations such as Operation *Character*, delivered exactly the sort of support Slim demanded of Special Forces. This was to assist the work of the main, or conventional, forces by gathering close target reconnaissance and mounting attacks on enemy rear echelons, lines of communications and other such 'soft' targets by means of ambushes and hit-and-run raids. Without the operations of these SOE-led Karen guerrillas in blocking the Japanese 56th Division's attempts to defend Toungoo and 18th Division's efforts to reinforce it, Fourteenth Army would almost certainly have been stopped in its tracks. If this had happened, it is reasonable to surmise that Kimura would not have felt the need to evacuate Rangoon, with all the attendant difficulties for Operation *Dracula* of having to assault a defended capital just as the monsoon struck. The estimate of Japanese killed by Operation *Character* was 11,874, far more than those killed by the soldiers of IV Corps and XXXIII Corps. As Richard Duckett rightly asserts, Operation *Character* achieved dramatic operational effect at 'a low cost in terms of men and equipment' by helping 'to protect the flank of Slim's XIV Army as it advanced into southern Burma … [By] raising the local population and operating in difficult terrain, the *Character* teams assisted regular forces by inflicting significant casualties upon the Japanese, as well as psychological damage.'

With Toungoo secured, XXXIII Corps pressed hard down the Irrawaddy, breaking the western end of Kimura's defence line. With Kimura distracted by Toungoo, Evans' 7th Indian Division struck at Yenangyaung on 22 April, before driving forcefully along the road to Prome. Simultaneously, Gracey's 20th Indian Division took Taungdwingyi in a surprise attack, thwarting any escape by the remnants of Sakurai's Twenty-Eighth Army over the Pegu Yoma, thus preventing their involvement in the battle for Toungoo. On 2 May Prome fell.

It was the loss of Toungoo that persuaded Kimura that he could not hold Rangoon. He needed to get the bulk of his army onto the eastern side of Pegu to offer them any hope of fighting a battle for Sittang and Tenasserim. Accordingly, he rushed up troops of divisional strength to defend Toungoo just as 17th Indian Division – veterans of the 1942 retreat – and the Shermans of 255th Tank Brigade arrived. On 29 April Cowan's division reached the town and cut it off from the Sittang, two brigades crossing the river despite Japanese bridge demolitions and strong resistance. Cowan's arrival in the town coincided with that of the monsoon rains. The Japanese defence collapsed, and Cowan's triumphant division now turned right and made its way towards Rangoon.

With 17th Indian Division making slow progress through the rain and mud from the north-east, Operation *Dracula* was launched from Akyab

and Ramree islands on 2 May, with Major-General Chamber's 26th Indian Division landing in two assault waves onto both sides of the Rangoon River, and Gurkhas of 50th Indian Parachute Brigade jumping on Elephant Point and squashing the resistance provided by the small garrison. It was a measure of the technical and logistical power of the Allies that this assault was organized and launched in less than a month. If ever there was a statement of overwhelming superiority, this was it. Six convoys delivered the troops, covered in the air by No. 224 Group, four escort aircraft carriers, eight squadrons of the Strategic Air Force and four squadrons of the US 12th Bombardment Group. At sea the convoy was protected by two battleships (*Queen Elizabeth* and *Richelieu*), a further two escort aircraft carriers, three cruisers and six destroyers. The Japanese had no answer to this overwhelming display of military power at sea, in the air or on land. Nevertheless, the amphibious assault proved precarious, as the arrival of the invasion convoys coincided with the arrival of a cyclone from the Bay of Bengal, only superlative seamanship enabling the operation to take place as planned. As the operation got underway, aerial reconnaissance of Rangoon Gaol showed that POWs had written 'Extract Digit' on the roof of one of the building's wings, suggesting that the Japanese had left the city, a fact that was confirmed shortly thereafter when an RAF aircraft landed at Mingaladon and the pilot hitch-hiked into the city. The first rain-sodden troops of 26th Indian Division entered the hastily vacated city the following day, contacting troops of XXXIII Corps and IV Corps on the roads to Prome and Pegu respectively on 6 May. *Dracula* had proved to be an essential part of the strategy for recovering Burma. Fourteenth Army could not have secured Rangoon, and recovered its port functionality by means of a land advance from Mandalay and Meiktila by XXXIII and IV Corps alone.

Operation *Dracula*, 1–7 May 1945

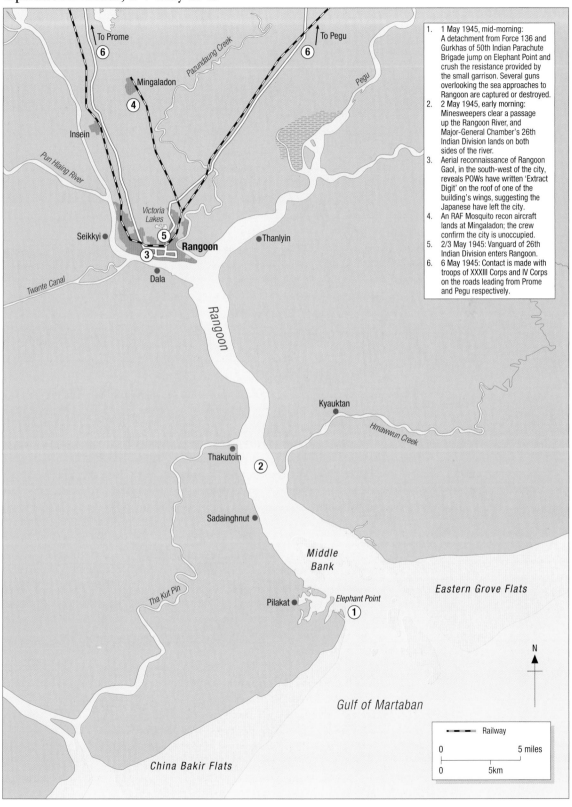

1. 1 May 1945, mid-morning: A detachment from Force 136 and Gurkhas of 50th Indian Parachute Brigade jump on Elephant Point and crush the resistance provided by the small garrison. Several guns overlooking the sea approaches to Rangoon are captured or destroyed.
2. 2 May 1945, early morning: Minesweepers clear a passage up the Rangoon River, and Major-General Chamber's 26th Indian Division lands on both sides of the river.
3. Aerial reconnaissance of Rangoon Gaol, in the south-west of the city, reveals POWs have written 'Extract Digit' on the roof of one of the building's wings, suggesting the Japanese have left the city.
4. An RAF Mosquito recon aircraft lands at Mingaladon; the crew confirm the city is unoccupied.
5. 2/3 May 1945: Vanguard of 26th Indian Division enters Rangoon.
6. 6 May 1945: Contact is made with troops of XXXIII Corps and IV Corps on the roads leading from Prome and Pegu respectively.

AFTERMATH

THE BATTLE OF THE BREAKOUT

Rangoon was quickly transformed into the focal point for the next phase of anticipated SEAC operations against Japan – Operations *Zipper* and *Mailfist*, the invasion of Malaya and Singapore, planned for September. But the capture of Rangoon did not mean that the whole of Burma was now in Allied hands. Kimura's troops still held significant pockets in the east and south-east, with at least two groups of troops, amounting to perhaps 15,000 men of Sakurai's Twenty-Eighth Army, in the Irrawaddy Valley and the hills of the Pegu Yoma bypassed in Fourteenth Army's rush south, together with 6,000 men in the Shan Hills to the east of Meiktila. Kimura's plan was to concentrate what forces he had on the Sittang and the Salween Valley – about 25,000 men of Honda's Thirty-Third Army – together with another 25,000 in the area of Moulmein. He was hopeful that the newly arrived monsoon would be his friend, and allow most of the troops isolated north of Toungoo to move through the hills to safety in Thailand. But operations between early June and 6 August, in what became known as the Battle of the Breakout, demonstrated the complete mastery by the Allies of the battlefield, and resulted in the destruction of large numbers of Japanese soldiers attempting to move to safety across the Sittang. The British knew that the Japanese were going to attempt to break out across the Sittang, helped by the capture on 2 July by a Gurkha patrol of a briefcase containing the entire Japanese plans for the operation. When the attempts by Thirty-Third Army to escape began, on 3 July, heavy artillery and ground-attack fire decimated the Japanese columns, and the attempt was called off on 7 July. On 15 July the Twenty-Eighth Army began their attempt to breakout, but were likewise caught in carefully planned killing fields by artillery, tanks and air power. Despite Japanese bravery and determination, it proved a one-sided battle. In the last significant land battle of World War II, the Japanese lost some 14,000 men.

In a sign that Japanese morale had reached rock bottom, an unprecedented 740 soldiers surrendered in the month to 4 August, during which time at least 6,270 had been killed. Ironically, the atomic bombs dropped on Hiroshima and Nagasaki that led to the Japanese surrender on 15 August did more than anything to preserve the unnecessary slaughter of Japanese lives in the Far East. Even under more enlightened commanders, such as Kimura, Japanese generalship still depended, when things weren't going well, on the lemming-like sacrifice of its soldiers to shore up poor decisions by its commanders.

Japanese breakout operations, Pegu Yoma, July 1945

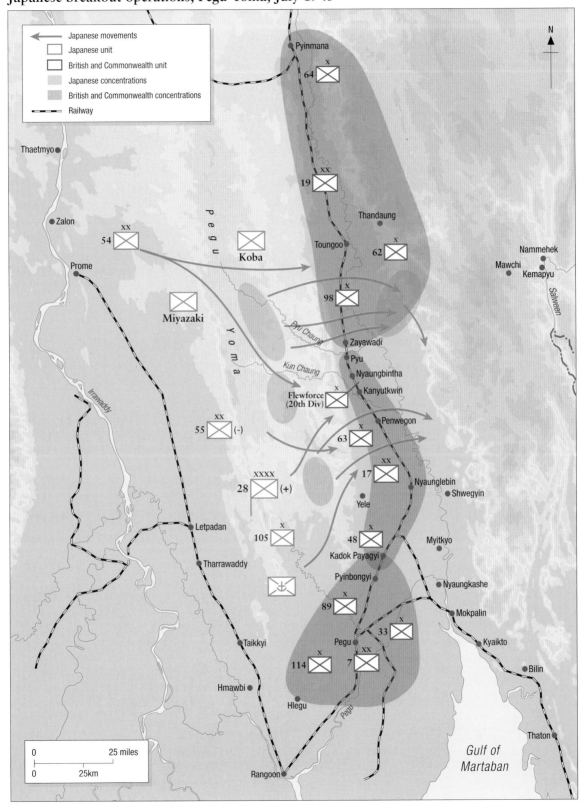

Note: gridlines are shown at intervals of 2km (1.24 miles)

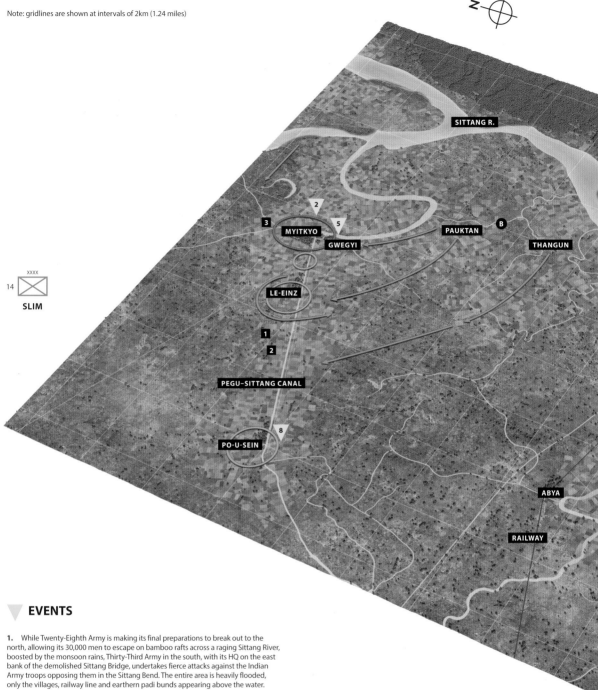

SITTANG R.

MYITKYO

GWEGYI

PAUKTAN

THANGUN

LE-EINZ

14 SLIM

PEGU–SITTANG CANAL

PO-U-SEIN

ABYA

RAILWAY

▼ EVENTS

1. While Twenty-Eighth Army is making its final preparations to break out to the north, allowing its 30,000 men to escape on bamboo rafts across a raging Sittang River, boosted by the monsoon rains, Thirty-Third Army in the south, with its HQ on the east bank of the demolished Sittang Bridge, undertakes fierce attacks against the Indian Army troops opposing them in the Sittang Bend. The entire area is heavily flooded, only the villages, railway line and earthern padi bunds appearing above the water.

2. The 89th Brigade of 7th Indian Division holds the villages of Myitkyo, Nyaungkashe and Satthwagyon.

3. On the night of 3 July all three villages come under heavy fire from Japanese artillery. Japanese guns focus especially on the village of Nyaungkashe, held by two companies of 4th/8th Gurkha Rifles.

4. On the same night, the Japanese launch an attack on the village of Satthwagyon, but are driven off by an immediate counter-attack by 1st/11th Sikhs.

5. The Japanese launch attacks against both Myitkyo and Nyaungkashe, but 89th Brigade holds firm.

6. The RAF mounts attacks on Japanese artillery locations, despite the low visibility in the monsoon, but heavy Japanese artillery fire continues against Nyaungkashe. The Gurkhas, unable to dig in because of the flooded terrain, suffer many casualties.

7. On 7 July, with casualties mounting, the GOC 7th Indian Division orders 4th/8th Gurkhas to withdraw from Nyaungkashe to Satthwagyon. One of its forward platoons, with three Vickers machine guns of the 13th Frontier Force Machine-Gun Battalion, hold a position on the west bank of the Sittang Bridge. It comes under constant fire all day. Its three guns are knocked out and only seven men survive, five of whom are wounded. The Japanese Thirty-Third Army still holds a sting in its tale right to the end.

8. The 3rd/6th Gurkha Rifles at Myitkyo are withdrawn two miles to the south-west along the Pegu–Sittang canal, where they can be better supplied.

9. The Japanese then occupy both Myitkyo and Nyaungkashe. They undertake several aggressive patrols in the weeks that follow, until a final encounter with men of the 1st Queens Royal Regiment on 27 July brings to an end the Japanese attempts to dominate the bend. A last attack on Satthwagyon on 2 August is the final act in the battle of the Sittang Bend.

JAPANESE THIRTY-THIRD ARMY ATTACKS IN THE SITTANG BEND, JULY 1945

The Japanese, defeated in Burma by Slim's strike at Toungoo and capture of Rangoon in May, did not believe in surrender, and made plans in July and August to withdraw the surviving 30,000 troops of the Burma Area Army east across the Sittang River, between Toungoo in the north and Mokpalin (the site of the famous bridge demolished by the British in 1942) in the south. It was a desperate venture by the Japanese, and arguably an unnecessary battle, as it was one-sided, the Allies inflicting very considerable casualties. About 14,000 Japanese soldiers died, for fewer than 100 Allied. Yet the Japanese continued to fight fiercely, and bravely. Here, troops of the Thirty-Third Army in the south-east undertake a diversionary attack towards units of the Fourteenth Army in the Waw–Sittang Bend region of the Pegu–Sittang canal, west of the village of Myitkyo, between 7 and 10 July 1945. Men of the Kan-I Group (4,350-strong) were due to cross to the north of Myitkyo.

MAJOR JAPANESE UNITS
A. Thirty-Third Army
B. 53rd Division (2,000-strong)
C. 18th Division (3,000-strong)

MAJOR ALLIED UNITS
1. 7th Indian Division
2. 89th Indian Infantry Brigade, 7th Indian Division
3. 3rd/6th Gurkha Rifles, 89th Indian Infantry Brigade
4. 4th/8th Gurkha Rifles, 89th Indian Infantry Brigade
5. 1st/11th Sikhs, 89th Indian Infantry Brigade
6. 13th Frontier Force Machine-Gun Battalion, 7th Indian Division
   33rd Indian Infantry Brigade, 7th Indian Division
   1st Queen's Royal Regiment, 33rd Indian Brigade
   4th/15th Punjab Regiment, 33rd Indian Brigade
   4th/1st Gurkha Rifles, 33rd Indian Brigade

RAF Liberators bomb a Japanese train on the Pegu to Moulmein railway line in Burma, June 1945. The train was carrying retreating Japanese troops and oil supplies. (Mirrorpix via Getty Images)

By the end of the campaign, the Imperial Japanese Army had lost 185,149 dead in Burma; the Allies a fraction of that in what was otherwise a nasty, brutal war – a mere 14,326 dead, by contrast. Japan had demonstrated that it was good at killing: it allowed more of its own troops to die for their country than it managed to kill of its enemy. They were particularly good at killing prisoners of war and the civilians of the countries they so egregiously absorbed into their ill-gotten empire.

THE BATTLEFIELDS TODAY

When the political situation in Myanmar (formerly Burma) allows, it is relatively easy to explore most of the battlefields described in this book, although a good local guide who can arrange the requisite logistics and smooth any political sensibilities is essential. Many places, such as the Karenni and the Kachin hills, are not merely remote, but politically sensitive, and it is not advisable to travel without good local knowledge. Large swathes of these regions, as well as Arakan in the west and Shan State in the east, have been off-limits to international travellers for years. To travel in some other parts of the country a permit is required as well as a locally licensed tour guide. To help travellers navigate themselves through these requirements, I recommend high-quality, locally based travel organizations, such as Sampan Travel (www.sampantravel.com), as they are able to access local expertise,

Japanese prisoners of war are washed by Lance-Corporal Smith after being captured during the last stages of the Japanese breakthrough along the Toungoo–Pegu road in their attempt to reach Thailand, 10 August 1945. (Mirrorpix via Getty Images)

as well as ensure that revenue stays in country and enable journeys to have a beneficial impact on the lives of local communities.

Many of the places mentioned in this book remain very similar to how they would have looked in 1944–45. Certainly, across many of the battlefields, from Kalewa to Mandalay, Meiktila and Toungoo, one can easily determine the shape of the battle despite development, including new roads and housing. There are many places where no development has taken place since the war and the ground is as one would have found it then.

The Chindwin, Irrawaddy and Sittang still carve their majestic ways through the country, and are obvious anchors for the traveller. But distances are considerable: it's easy to become complacent about how long it might take to get from A to B, without taking into account the fact that apart from the new roads from Yangon (formerly Rangoon) to Mandalay, and to Mawlamyine (formerly Moulmein), most roads remain essential economic links between towns and villages, and are therefore slow.

To travel over the border of Myanmar into India or China is possible, but tricky. The assistance of locally based organizations is essential and travellers should begin planning their crossing well in advance so to have the best chance possible of jumping through the required bureaucratic hoops in time.

Japanese prisoners of war in a Rangoon compound in August 1945. (Mirrorpix via Getty Images)

Most travellers begin their journey in Yangon. The city offers an excellent start point, with a wide range of high-quality accommodation and facilities. Yangon itself has considerable historic interest and demands a stay – if one can afford the time – of at least several days. From Yangon it is possible to travel south by car to Kyaikto, Hpa-An and Mawlamyine (Moulmein). To the latter there is also a scenic railway through rural Mon villages and thick forest. However, as is the case with all train travel in Myanmar, it is a slow and bumpy journey. There are also air links south to Tavoy and Victoria Point in Tenasserim.

From Yangon it is possible to drive along the old highway to Taungoo (Toungoo) or up to Mandalay on the new highway. There are regular flights between Yangon and Mandalay as well as another slow and bumpy train. From Mandalay, travel can be undertaken north to Myitkyina by rail or air. From Myitkyina travellers can journey west to Mogaung, Indawgyi Lake and other sites of Operation *Thursday*. Travelling east by road or rail from Mandalay, it is possible to reach the Gokteik Viaduct (a Chindit target in Operation *Longcloth* in 1943) and then onto Lashio and the China border.

The beaches of southern Arakan are easy to access by flight or along the road from Yangon. However, the northern districts of Buthidaung and Maungdaw up on the border with Bangladesh are almost impossible for international travellers to enter.

The Irrawaddy and Chindwin are easily navigable and offer attractive tourist routes up or down river. At the height of the dry season, however, as this author can attest, the Irrawaddy can get quite low, and make mid-river strandings not just possible, but probable. Again, reputable travel agencies can take the hassle out of guessing from afar. Travelling the Irrawaddy with a good map and a good boat captain is an excellent way to find and visit the various crossing points. The journey upriver to Kalewa is generally only possible during the wet season.

Travellers will discover that knowledge of World War II in Myanmar is slight. Communities living upon battlefields are often unaware of their significance. However, any good local guide worth their salt will know who to speak to in order to ferret out any remaining secrets or – if you are very lucky – surviving first-hand accounts. In recent years travellers have met villagers in Indawgyi who remember aircraft crashing into the lake and farmers outside Mawlamyine who have vague memories of the construction of the Burma Death Railway.

Although in modern Myanmar there is a dearth of knowledge – and indeed, interest – in World War II, there is great pride in seeing any foreigner take an interest in their country. People are keen to assist where they can – eager to help iron out the creases of a journey and make a visit to the battlefields as enjoyable and fruitful as possible.

BIBLIOGRAPHY

Allen, Louis, *Burma: The Longest War* (London: Dent, 1984)

Bond, Brian (ed.), *British and Japanese Military Leadership in the Far Eastern War, 1941–1945* (London: Cass, 2004)

Brett-James, Anthony, *Ball of Fire: The Fifth Indian Division in the Second World War* (Aldershot: Gale and Polden, 1951)

Callahan, Raymond and Daniel Marston, *The 1945 Burma Campaign and the Transformation of the British Indian Army* (Lawrence, Kansas: University of Kansas Press, 2021)

Drea, Edward, *In the Service of the Emperor: Essays on the Imperial Japanese Army* (Lincoln and London: University of Nebraska Press, 1998)

Duckett, Richard, *The Special Operations Executive in Burma* (London: I.B. Tauris, 2018)

Latimer, Jon, *Burma: The Forgotten War* (London: John Murray, 2005)

Lyman, Robert, *Slim: Master of War* (London: Constable, 2004)

Lyman, Robert, *A War of Empires* (Oxford: Osprey Publishing Ltd, 2021)

MacDonald Fraser, George, *Quartered Safe Out Here* (London: Harvill, 1992)

Mountbatten of Burma, Admiral the Earl, *Report to the Combined Chiefs of Staff, 1943–1945* (London: HMSO, 1951)

Nair, K.S., *The Forgotten Few: The Indian Air Force in World War II* (Noida, UP, India: HarperCollins, 2019)

Prasad, Bisheshwar (ed.), *Official History of the Indian Army Forces in the Second World War: Campaigns in the Eastern Theatre*, Vol. II: *Reconquest of Burma* (Calcutta: Orient Longmans, 1958)

Probert, Henry, *The Forgotten Air Force: The Royal Air Force in the War against Japan, 1941–1945* (London: Brassey's, 1995)

Roberts, Michael, *Golden Arrow: The Story of the 7th Indian Division* (Aldershot: Gale and Polden, 1952)

Slim, William J., *Defeat into Victory* (London: Cassell, 1956)

Tamayama, Kazuo and John Nunneley, *Tales by Japanese Soldiers of the Burma Campaign 1942–45* (London: Cassell, 2000)

Thompson, Julian, *The Imperial War Museum Book of the War in Burma 1942–1945* (London: Pan, 2002)

Woodburn Kirby, Stanley, *The War against Japan*, Vol. IV: *The Reconquest of Burma* (London: HMSO, 1965)

Young, Edward, *Meiktila 1945* (Oxford: Osprey Publishing Ltd, 2004)

INDEX

Figures in **bold** refer to illustrations.